EDGAR CAYCE

ON JESUS AND HIS CHURCH

BY ANNE READ

Under the editorship of Hugh Lynn Cayce

WARNER

PAPERBACK LIBRARY
NEW YORK

WARNER PAPERBACK LIBRARY EDITION

First Printing: September, 1970
Second Printing: November, 1971
Third Printing: December, 1971
Fourth Printing: November, 1972

Warner Paperback Library is a division of Warner Books, Inc.,
315 Park Avenue South, New York, N.Y. 10010.

EDGAR CAYCE ON JESUS AND HIS CHURCH

Many people for whom Edgar Cayce gave life readings were surprised to learn that in an earlier incarnation their lives had been intimately connected with that of Jesus—from the teenaged daughter of the Bethlehem innkeeper who turned Mary and Joseph away with the words "No room at the inn," to the Holy Women who 33 years later sat anguished at the foot of the cross.

In this moving and beautiful book, Anne Read weaves together such records into a richly detailed supplement to the New Testament account of the life, death and resurrection of Jesus who became the Christ.

INTRODUCTION

EDGAR CAYCE ON JESUS AND HIS CHURCH
For Anne Read, her Bible came alive again as she read the Edgar Cayce readings on Jesus and the people of His time. In *Edgar Cayce On Jesus And His Church,* she passes on to her readers her excitement and the new insight she discovered for herself. This book is not a scholarly treatise; nor is it a copy of the readings. It is a layman's, a gifted housewife's, study of and reaction to Edgar Cayce's psychic data on the life and times of Jesus.

Perhaps it was because Edgar Cayce himself loved the Bible so (he read it completely through once every year of his life) that his unconscious used Biblical language in his discourses and frequently quoted or paraphrased Biblical passages as illustrations. As a Sunday school teacher, Edgar Cayce worked with both children and adults throughout his lifetime wherever he lived—Kentucky, Alabama, Ohio and Virginia.

Thousands of persons who have now become familiar with the psychic data of this man, who has become known to many as the "Sleeping Prophet" from Jess Stearn's bestseller by that name, have said in letters and in person that the most valuable help they have secured lies in the area of a renewed interest and new understanding of the Bible.

This was true for Anne Read, who moved for a time with her family to Virginia Beach. It was the readings on Jesus which fascinated her. She read, copied and discussed these data. Later, I deliberately directed her interest to the diet material from the readings and asked her to do classes for our conferences on it. Out of this came a coauthorship of a booklet that includes many recipes based on the Edgar Cayce readings. This has been published by Paperback Library under the title *Edgar Cayce On Diet And Health.*

Anne Read's first love is the story of Jesus. Lucid, direct, warm, beautifully interwoven in a narrative form, Mrs. Read has used the readings from Edgar Cayce accurately and effectively in telling an exciting and in some ways new story of Jesus and his church.

For some of you, this may be the first introduction to Edgar Cayce. "Who was he?"

It depends on through whose eyes you look at him. A goodly number of his contemporaries knew the "waking" Edgar Cayce as a gifted professional photographer. Another group (predominately children) admired him as a warm and friendly Sunday school teacher. His own family knew him as a wonderful husband and father.

The "sleeping" Edgar Cayce was an entirely different figure—a psychic known to thousands of people in all walks of life, who had cause to be grateful for his help. Indeed, many of them believed that he alone had either saved or changed their lives when all seemed lost. The "sleeping" Edgar Cayce was a medical diagnostician, a prophet and a devoted proponent of Bible lore.

Even as a child, on a farm near Hopkinsville, Kentucky, where he was born on March 18, 1877, Edgar Cayce displayed powers of perception which seemed to extend beyond the normal range of the five senses. At the age of six or seven, he told his parents that he was able to see and talk to "visions"—sometimes of relatives who had reecntly died. His parents attributed this to the overactive imagination of a lonely child who had been influenced by the dramatic language of the revival meetings which were popular in that section of the country. Later, by sleeping with his head on his schoolbooks, he developed some form of photographic memory which helped him advance rapidly in the country school. This gift faded, however, and Edgar was only able to complete his seventh grade before he had to seek his own place in the world.

By the age of twenty-one, he had become the salesman for a wholesale stationery company. At this time he developed a gradual paralysis of the throat muscles which threatened the loss of his voice. When doctors were unable to find a physical cause for this condition, hypnosis was tried but it failed to have any permanent effect. As a last resort, Edgar asked a friend to help him re-enter the same kind of hypnotic sleep that had enabled him to memorize his schoolbooks as a child. His friend gave him the necessary suggestion and once he was in a self-induced trance, Edgar came to grips with his own problem. He recommended medication and manipulative therapy which successfully restored his voice and repaired his system.

A group of physicians from Hopkinsville and Bowling Green, Kentucky, took advantage of his unique talent to diagnose their own patients. They soon discovered that Cayce only needed to be given the name and address of a patient, wherever he was, to be able to tune in telepathically on that individual's mind and body as easily as if they were both in the same room. He needed, and was given, no other information regarding any patient.

One of the young M.D.'s, Dr. Wesley Ketchum, submitted a report on this unorthodox procedure to a clinical research society in Boston. On October 9, 1910, *The New York Times* carried two pages of headlines and pictures. From that day on, troubled people from all over the country sought help from the "wonder man."

When Edgar Cayce died on January 3, 1945, in Virginia Beach, Virginia, he left well over 14,000 documented stenographic records of the telepathic-clairvoyant statements he had given for more than 6,000 different people over a period of forty-three years. These documents are referred to as "readings."

The readings constitute one of the largest and most impressive records of psychic perception ever to emanate from a single individual. Together with their relevant records, correspondence and reports, they have been cross-indexed under thousands of subject headings and placed at the disposal of psychologists, students, writers and investigators who still come, in increasing numbers, to examine them.

A foundation known as the A.R.E. (Association for Research and Enlightenment, Inc., P. O. Box 595, Virginia Beach, Virginia 23451) was founded in 1932 to preserve these readings. As an open-membership research society, it continues to index and catalog the information, initiate investigation and experiments, and promote conferences, seminars and lectures. Until now, its published findings have been made available only to its members through its own publishing facilities.

————*Hugh Lynn Cayce*

PREFACE

A beautiful and meaningful story of the life of Jesus and his contemporaries may be pieced together from the fragments given here and there in the Cayce readings. It is the purpose of this book to present in a readable and comprehensible form, this story, along with a comparative study of the information given in the Bible, and the explanations from the Cayce readings of certain theological concepts and certain of Jesus' teachings.

While the Bible has been a "lamp unto my feet" since childhood, I have found, during my years of Biblical study, many questions arising in my mind which the Bible itself did not answer. I have found the answers to many of these in the Cayce readings. From the study of this material has come to me a new understanding and appreciation of the events of this period, and their significance. Therefore, this book is written in the hope that it may prove helpful to those who seek to better know and serve the Master, Jesus who became the Christ.

PART ONE

WHEN THE MASTER WALKED IN THE EARTH

CHAPTER ONE

JESUS WHO BECAME THE CHRIST

He lived, this man called Jesus, in one of the smallest, most insignificant of the Roman provinces. Although his name is known today throughout all the world, in his lifetime, two thousand years ago, he was virtually unknown outside his own province. He is worshipped today as the Son of God by a very large portion of the world's population, yet he died the death of a criminal. He changed the course of world history as no other man ever has, yet hardly a mention of him can be found in the history of his own time, unless the Bible be counted as history. He is the central figure of the New Testament, yet the New Testament is strangely silent about most of the years of his life.

When Edgar Cayce came on the scene in the present century, with his amazing ability to give answers while in a trance state to all kinds of questions, it was not at all strange that many individuals and groups should ask for more information concerning the life and times of Jesus. A wealth of information was given in answer to these requests. Furthermore, in a considerable number of the life readings (records of a person's previous incarnations) the record of a particular incarnation would begin with these words: "In the days when the Master walked in the earth . . ." Many of these individuals had, according to Cayce, been closely associated with Jesus, and the records of their own experiences furnish additional information concerning the period and the activities of Jesus and many of the events mentioned in the Bible, as well as valuable insight into the effects which their associations with the Prince of Peace had upon their lives and consciousness.

That such records exist and that it is possible to obtain such information of events long past through these is a concept that may be questionable to some. Cayce gave an explanation of "how an entity's or soul's records are made or kept, and how they may be read" as follows:

"Upon the skein of time and space are the records made. For thoughts and deeds are indeed things, and their currents run with time and space and make their impressions there; just as in the mental forces it is gradually being comprehended that as the man, as the being thinketh in his heart, so is he. Thus, as an entity dwells upon, as the entity turns within to meet its Maker and those promises that are living experiences, that may be read of self as to the manner in which ye abide in the life, in the word, the being of Him ye have beheld manifested in the flesh. As ye abide in Him, and He in the Father, ye have, then, those influences in thine inner self that make for that as He gave, 'There will be brought to thy remembrance all things from the foundations of the world that ye have need of in thine experience for the glorifying of the Father through the Son.' "

Such records, having been made available to us through the ability of a man who did "turn within to meet his Maker," may be the source of a much truer and more complete understanding of the life of Jesus than the Bible alone. Cayce suggests something of this by saying that

that which we speak of as "the record of the son of man as he walked in the earth" is the record made by those who would influence the religious and spiritual life of individuals, yet who never really knew him. He reminds us of how Jesus "made those inferences and illustrations as to how those closed their ears to what was actually going on about them."

The story of Jesus' life and its significance cannot be fully understood without understanding man's purpose on earth and the necessity for Jesus' entering the earth for his own part in the fulfillment of that purpose. Cayce explains this very concisely:

"He, our Lord," Cayce says, "was the first among those that put on mortality* that there might be the opportunity for those forces that had erred in spiritual things; and only through experiencing in the various phases as they developed through that ye know as matter could they come to know how or why or when there was made manifest in any realm spirit that was good, and spirit that was in error. . . ."

He came, this soul we know as Jesus, Cayce continued, in many different ages, as a spokesman to "manifest the first idea." These incarnations (or those of the incarnations mentioned in the Bible) were given as Adam, Enoch, Melhiizedek, Joseph, Joshua, Jeshua, and finally Jesus. Perhaps this would explain the apostle Paul's referring to Jesus as the "last Adam" in his statement, "As in the first Adam all die, so in the last Adam all are made alive."

Cayce explains the passage in the book of Job (which he states is an allegory, the story of mankind in the earth) where the Lord says to Satan, "He is in thine hand, but touch not his soul!" thus: "The coming into the earth has been and is for the evolving of the soul unto the awareness of the effect of all influences in its experience

---

* As Adam

13

in the varied spheres of activity." All this could only be overcome, he says, "in Him who was the creator, the maker, the experiencer of mortality and spirit and soul."

This soul who came as Jesus has come, Cayce says, "in all ages when it has been necessary for the understanding to be centered in new application of the same thought: 'God is Spirit, and seeks such to worship Him in spirit and in truth.'" By this Cayce is not referring, it appears, only to the times in which he appeared in an incarnate form. For, according to Cayce, "This entity, as an entity, influenced, either directly or indirectly, all these forms of philosophy or religious thought that taught God was One." For "in all of these there is that same impelling spirit."

Cayce frequently referred to the Master as "Jesus who became the Christ" and explained that "Jesus is the man —the activity, the mind, the relationships that He bore to others. Yea, He was mindful of friends, He was sociable, He was loving, He was kind, He was gentle. He grew faint, He grew weak, and yet gained that strength that He has promised, in becoming the Christ, by fulfilling and overcoming the world! Ye are made strong, in body, in mind, in soul and purpose, by that power in Christ. The *power* then, is in the Christ. The *pattern* is in Jesus." This is somewhat similar to the explanation that through the perfect application of the law one becomes the law, and as Jesus, the man, applied the law ("No doubt, no fear, no animosity, no self—but selfless in God's purpose") he made himself equal with the law by becoming the law.

The necessity, then, says Cayce, for the "entering in of Jesus" is this: "that there may come into the earth those influences that will save, regenerate, resuscitate, hold, if you please, the earth in its continued activity toward the proper understanding and proper relationships to . . . that which is in Him alone." For "has it not been said, has it not been shown in the experience of the earth, the world, from any angle it may be considered, that He has

14

not willed that any should be lost, but has prepared the way of escape in him, the Maker?"

Jesus is the pattern, the example, the model, "in that He as a man manifested in the flesh the ability of flesh to make fleshly desires one with the will of the spirit." Through knowing more of his activities in the earth and by seeing him through the eyes, the experiences, of those who knew him as he walked in the earth, perhaps there may come a change also in our consciousness, enabling us to worship God in spirit and in truth and to make a closer approach to His throne.

CHAPTER TWO

THE ESSENES AND THEIR PREPARATION
FOR THE MESSIAH

There is little indicated in either sacred or profane history, Cayce points out, "as to the preparation of the mother for that channel through which immaculate conception might take place." Matthew begins the story of the coming of the Messiah with the simple statement that Mary, his mother, before she had come together with her husband, was found to be with child of the Holy Ghost. Luke, the only other Gospel writer who records Jesus' birth, begins with the events of a few months earlier, the account of the birth of the forerunner, John, and also of the announcement of the angel to Mary that she would conceive the child who would be called the Son of God. Other than the prophecies in the Old Testament we are left with no more background than this for the most important event of all history.

We have no biblical record of the events of a long period of time preceding the birth of Jesus, since Malachi, the last book of the Old Testament, was written almost four hundred years earlier. Due to this fact it has been generally assumed that little of importance, from a religious or spiritual standpoint, was happening during that period, and that the advent of the Messiah at that time was totally unexpected and unprepared for. This, according to Cayce, was far from the truth.

"Ye say," said Cayce, "that there were those periods when for four hundred years little or nothing had happened in the experience of man as a revelation from the Father, or God, or from the sources of Light. What was it, then, that made the setting for the place and for the entering in of that consciousness in the earth that ye know as the Son of Man, the Jesus of Nazareth, the Christ on the cross? Did the darkness bring light? Did the wandering away from the thought of such bring the Christ into the earth? Rather, is this idea not a refutation of the common law that is present in spirit, mind and body: that like begets like? As was asked oft, 'Can any good thing come out of Nazareth?'

"Isn't it rather that there were those that ye hear little or nothing of in thy studies—the Essenes—who dedicated their lives, their minds, their bodies to a purpose, to a seeking for that which had been to them a promise of old? Were there not individuals—men and women—who dedicated their bodies that they might be channels through which such influences, such a body might come?"

At the time of this reading, long before the discovery of the Dead Sea Scrolls and the excavation of the ruins at Qumran, it is indeed true that most individuals had heard little or nothing of the Essenes. They are not mentioned at all in the Bible. Yet from the information concerning them given by Josephus, the Jewish historian, Pliny, a Roman naturalist, and Philo of Alexandria, there had been speculations by many scholars concerning a possible relationship between the Essenes and Christianity, some scholars even believing that Jesus himself had been an Essene.

Then the discovery in 1947 of the Dead Sea Scrolls, and the excavation, beginning in 1951, of the ruins at Qumran aroused widespread interest, even excitement, in many quarters and considerable controversy among the scholars, and we began to hear much more about the Essenes, for it seemed most likely to many scholars that this was the sect of the scrolls and the Qumran community. This is not conclusively proven, since the name of the sect was not mentioned in the writings of the scrolls. The basic principles, however, and the organization and rules of discipline of this sect, as revealed in these

17

writings, are in keeping with that described by Josephus, Philo and Pliny as those of the Essenes. And while it is not certain when, where or by whom the scrolls were originally written, it is generally agreed that they were placed in the caves in which they were found during the first century B. C. or the first half of the first century A. D., during which period the Essenes, according to the historians, lived in the area. It is also agreed that the scrolls were undoubtedly the religious literature of the sect whose communal building was uncovered at Qumran, which geographical location agrees with that which Pliny gives as the place where the Essenes lived.

Much of the controversy which has raged around the scrolls has centered largely on the old question: Do they indicate a connection between the Essenes and Christianity? Much evidence has been given by some scholars in support of this theory. Much of this has been countered by conflicting evidence. That there were great similarities between the teachings and rituals of the Essenes and those of Christianity is certain. Perhaps the most commonly accepted theory, at least that of many writers, is that early Christianity was influenced by the beliefs of the Essenes, if, indeed, this is the identity of the Qumran sect, and that the scrolls furnish a picture of the religious and cultural climate in which John the Baptist conducted his mission and in which Jesus was initially reared. We shall see how well this agrees with the account given by Cayce.

The Essene community which played the most important part in the preparation for the coming of the Messiah, according to Cayce, was not that one in the desert of Judea, near the shores of the Dead Sea, but rather that group on Mount Carmel, the original place where the school of the prophets had been established during Elijah's time. This was only one of a number of such groups, apparently both in Palestine and in other countries, though it would seem, from the Cayce readings, that this community on Carmel was the main "headquarters" of the Essenes, since the Essene temple was situated here. Also there were many of the Essenes, or in Cayce's words, "the near adherents of same," who were not a part of the rigid monastic order and did not live in these communities but, though holding to the Essene beliefs and cooperating with their purposes and objectives, maintained private homes in various villages and towns.

It might be well, before going further with the account of the Essenes and their activities, to review the religious situation of which the Essenes were a part. Cayce furnishes us with a concise and graphic account of the different religious influences among the people of Palestine of this period, most of which may be verified through historical sources. The major groups, he says, holding to the orthodox Jewish belief, were the Sadducees and the Pharisees, those frequently referred to in the New Testament. These held to the "law and the prophets," or the ancient Hebrew scriptures containing the Mosaic law and the writings of the prophets of old, "as the way of acceptance and grace in the spiritual sense." The Samaritans, the mixed group resulting from the intermarriage of the Jews left in the land at the time of the Babylonian exile with the people of the conquerors who were brought in to inhabit the region, also held to the Mosaic law, and felt they were as well versed in it as the other groups, but there was a great difference in the manner in which the law was interpreted by their teachers and the way it was interpreted by the ministers and teachers of the synagogues of the more orthodox groups. There was also a great deal of influence on the people of that place and time of the religious beliefs of the Grecian and Roman peoples who "held to the idea of glorifying the body itself as a channel through which there might be sought manifestation by the divine, if there was a choice made by the divine—or if there were the divine, according to their reasoning." Then there were the Essenes, who, while sincere in their

19

purpose and while holding also to the Mosaic law, were so different in their beliefs and the activities of daily life from any of the first mentioned groups that they were considered by many, especially of the Pharisees, as rebels or radicals.

The Essenes were students of what we would call astrology, numerology, phrenology, and the study of the return of individuals, which is now called reincarnation, but which, Cayce says, was referred to as resurrection in those periods. This belief, being in direct conflict with the belief of the Sadducees, brought about persecution of the Essenes by these, who, being the wealthy, aristocratic families, the high priest and officials of the temple, had considerable authority.

While the other Jewish sects apparently no longer believed in the possibility of receiving revelations or guidance from the Divine, except through the law and prophets of old, this seems to have been one of the important tenets and interests of the Essenes, for, says Cayce, "These Essenes had cherished not merely the conditions that had come as word of mouth, but had kept the records of the periods when individuals had been visited with the supernatural, or out of the ordinary experiences, whether in dreams, visions, voices, or any of such experiences throughout the experiences of this peculiar people, which were felt by those students to be as promises, and the many ways these had been interpreted by those to whom the preservation of same had been committed. For they, the Essenes, taught the mysteries of man and his relationships to those forces as might be manifest from within and without."

Perhaps the chief characteristic of the Essenes, however, which distinguished them from the other sects of the time was their expectancy of the coming of the Messiah, and their making that expectancy an active part of their experience. Indeed, it was the chief reason for their existence. The name "Essene," according to Cayce, meant "expectancy." And it was their belief, their hope, their ideal, that through a stricter adherence to both the letter and the spirit of the law they might so purify themselves that it would be possible, through them, for the Promised One to enter into the earth.

In many lands, according to Cayce, "there was the looking, hoping, watching, seeking to know the time when the changes were to take place, the new order of things, the new cycle, the dawn of the new era, but in the Holy Land itself, where man, as man, had been looked upon as the only correct line of understanding or application, and woman, as an individual, was only to obey the master of the house, there had come that understanding of 'and the seed of the woman shall bruise his head.'" This, of course, refers to the statement in Genesis concerning the serpent, the evil one. Apparently, only here among the Essenes in the Holy Land was it recognized that the new era was to be ushered in with the birth of the child who was to be the Messiah of God, promised to Israel as that influence against evil which would be their salvation.

The people of that land of Israel had long looked for, longed for, the coming of the promised deliverer whom they expected to free them from bondage, lead them to victory over all their enemies, and set up a government which would bring peace and prosperity to all as individuals and raise them as a nation to a position of glory and prominence. And now they suffered under a double burden from which they longed for relief. For they were not only under bondage to Rome, with the necessity of paying heavy taxes to a hated conqueror, but also were oppressed by a corrupt priesthood who "gormandized themselves and their own interests in the sale of privileges in the activities of those things that were the letter of the law without the spirit thereof." And now, the Essenes believed, the time of their deliverance was drawing very near. For through astrology and numerology, at which the Essenes were adept, and which enabled them to proclaim a certain period as a cycle, it had been determined from the position of the North or Polar Star in relation to the southern clouds that there had come the beginning of the Piscean age, those periods when there were to be the changes in the order of things.

The preparations of the Essenes then entered a new phase. For while all of that brotherhood had joined in their efforts to so dedicate, so consecrate their lives that they, as a group, might provide the means through which the Son of Man might, through choice, enter into materiality, it seemed the time had now come to choose and prepare, through an especially strict discipline, a more concentrated effort, a number of girls with the hope, the purpose, that from them one might be selected to become the mother of the Messiah.

All the parents of young girls who were perfect in body and mind, who chose to dedicate their children for this service, brought them to the temple, or school, there on Mount Carmel where there were the priests of this faith. Twelve maidens were chosen from the initial group as most fit to dedicate, consecrate their bodies, their minds, their service to become a channel through which the Prince of Peace might come, that there might be, through the expression of that being in the earth, the understanding that the law was written in the hearts of men, rather than upon tables of stone; that the temple, that the holy of holies was to be within. The choice was made by the priests according to the selections indicated by the spirit.

Among those maidens presented at the temple was Mary, a child of four, the daughter of Ann. Ann was an unmarried woman who claimed that her child had been immaculately conceived. This claim, though true, was not believed, and the doubt as to Mary's parentage produced a division among the priests or leaders of the Essene

22

group, some feeling that it was not proper for such a child to be among those chosen for such a holy purpose; yet, because of the perfection of her body and mind, others felt the presentation could not be refused, and eventually Mary was among those chosen—"twelve in all," Cayce says, "as representatives of the twelve phases that had made up Israel, or man."

The training and preparation of the twelve by those of the Essene priesthood began while the maidens were yet children. It was not stated by Cayce whether or not these children were separated from their parents and lived together at the school. However, it was evident from the discoveries at Qumran that the members of this Essene community lived in tents or booths clustered around the communal building, but partook of common meals in this building, which was also the place where the daily activities of many of the members took place. It is probable that something of the same arrangement was in effect among those at Carmel. Certainly, according to Cayce, all phases of the activity of the girls was closely supervised. The training must have been, from his description, quite similar to that of present-day novices in some of the Roman Catholic religious orders. This seems especially likely in view of the fact that Cayce, in one reading, referring to the group of the Essenes as the lodge or church, adds, "for this is the church that is called the Catholic now . . . and is the closest."

"They were trained," Cayce says, "as to physical exercise first; trained as to mental exercises as related to chastity, purity, love, patience, endurance. All of these by what would be termed by many in the present as persecutions, but were as tests for physical and mental; and this was under the supervision of those that cared for the nourishments by the protection in food values. This was the manner in which they were trained, directed and protected. As to diet, no fermented drink was ever given. There were special foods; these were kept in

23

balance according to that which had been first set by Aron and Ra Ta* in Egypt."

So, during those early years, during the childhood of Mary, there were the continued preparation and dedication of those who might be the channel through whom might come that beloved Son, who would make the paths straight, and bring light out of darkness.

The Essene groups in the land of Palestine were not alone in the expectation of the coming of the Holy One. For, said Cayce, "In all lands where man sought to understand and know his relationship with creative forces there were those who looked for the day, the hour, when that great purpose, that event, was to be in the earth a literal experience."

The knowledge and understanding of what was to come to pass, and when and where, was apparently not a simple matter of one individual or even of one group being given a direct revelation, with complete details, but the result of painstaking study of and compilation of different bits of knowledge from many sources. There was, as might be expected among those of high spiritual ideals and purposes, a great deal of cooperation among the different groups as to the exchange of information, and a banding together "of those of various groups through one channel or another . . . to study the material which was handed down through the varied groups in that day and period." Cayce tells of many of these individuals through whom the information was given and how it was shared with those of other groups.

The individual most important in this portion of the story is a woman named Judy, "the first of women," ac-

---

*Ra Ta was a prophet or priest among a group from the Caucasian mountains which invaded Egypt about 11000 B. C. He became High Priest of Egypt and directed the building of the Temple of Sacrifice for purposes of aiding in the physical evolution of man, and the Temple Beautiful for spiritual development and vocational training. (from E. C. reading #294)

cording to Cayce, "appointed as the head of the Essenes group, who had the experience of hearing voices, as well as those which would be called in the present experience communications with the influences which had been a part of man's experience from the beginning, such that the divine within man heard the experiences of those forces outside of man, and communicated in voices, in dreams, in signs and symbols which had become a portion of the experience."

That a woman should have been appointed as the head of the Essenes during that period of history, when women were generally considered as being definitely inferior to men, seems quite strange. Judy, however, was obviously a very unusual woman; indeed her story is unusual from its beginning.

Judy's parents, Phinehas and his wife Elkatma, were among the Essenes at Carmel. Some twenty-four years before the birth of Jesus they had had an experience similar to that of Hanna and Elkanah, the parents of the prophet Samuel, to whom a child was promised whose life was to be dedicated to the Lord. There had been an appearance (supposedly by an angel), said Cayce, to first the mother and then to the father, informing each "as to what should be the ministry, the activity, of this entity," and the "glorious work" she was to perform. Apparently, however, there was no indication given that the child was to be a girl. For when she was born, the fact that the child was a daughter rather than a son, Cayce says, "brought some disturbance, some confusion in the minds of many." The parents, however, still holding to their faith in the experiences they had had and the promises concerning the child which they had received, dedicated the life of their child, Judy, to the study of "those things that had been handed down as a part of the experiences of those who had received visitations from the unseen, the unknown, or that worshiped as the Divine Spirit moving into the activities of man."

Judy was brought up with that training, those disciplines, that were considered by these people to be conducive to the development of psychic or prophetic abilities. Her studies included not only the prophecies and traditions of her own people, but also those from all the teachings of the East, the traditions from India, Egypt, and "the Persian lands and the borders about same." She was apparently very impressed by the fact that much of this teaching, or the experiences of these peoples, was handed down as oral tradition rather than as written records, and much of her studies and activities were devoted to the effort to record this information and to learning the best methods for preserving these records for future generations. Judy became, then, not only a prophet and healer but also a teacher and recorder, and these studies and activities made her remarkably well qualified for her future work. For eventually, having been appointed by this time as the head of the Essenes, she was active in compiling, for the study of her own group, the information resulting from the studies of the groups of other lands, as well as her own, as related to the coming of the promised one.

One of those of Judy's own group, the Essenes of Carmel, through whom such information came was a woman named Anna. She was, said Cayce, "among those who sought, through the mysteries of the sages, to interpret time and place according to the stars and the numerological effects upon the period." Apparently, although the Essenes as a whole were a dedicated group, there were some associated with them who had selfish motives, and attempted to use information obtained from Anna for material gains. This created some disturbance among the group. Also, with the realization that selfish use was being made of her work, "there was brought the desire," Cayce said, "to hide self's knowledge away, without giving expression of same to all the seekers of those groups."

Shalmar was one of the Essenes who were active in

gathering data from the teachers of various lands. He was one of the sages associated with the priests in the Carmelian area, and was acquainted, Cayce says, "with the teachings of those groups in Persia, India, Egypt, and even of the Hebrews and the activities in Olympus and the isles of the sea." He and the prophetess Anna were among those through whom the choice was made of the twelve maidens for their preparation.

There were those, also, who came to Carmel from other lands for consultation with the Essenes there, bringing with them that which had been received through their own insights or efforts. One such visitor from other lands —who became, indeed, more than a visitor—was a woman, a prophetess called Zermada.

Zermada was, as Cayce expressed it, "in keeping and the application of spiritual tenets of the Syrophoenician peoples." She had been a student of astrology from her early years, and developed also ability "as a dreamer, as a mediator, as a seeress or prophetess," and had been associated with the people of the Far East. Having come to the conclusion, early in her experience, through her own studies and abilities, that the looked-for changes were coming in the Holy or Promised Land, Zermada made many journeys to that area, and finally came to dwell in the community on Carmel, although apparently not as an actual member of the group, for, Cayce says, although Zermada and Judy "counseled together oft," each had her own inner group, and each considered herself an authority in or among her own particular group, and the findings of each were more fully accepted by her own group than by the others. However, there was kept a "bond of purposefulness between the two," for each realized that there must be less of self, that their common purpose was more important than their individual desires for self-exaltation.

Many people of other lands came to the Holy land to consult with Zermada, especially when, through her associations with Judy, there came more communications and more interpretations of the records or signs already known of by these "wise men" of the East. For, according to Cayce, there was more than one visit of those called the "wise men," some coming from "Persia, India, and the Egyptian land to Carmel, seeking for more knowledge of that which was to come to pass. They reasoned with the Brethren, but more was sought from the studies of the woman, Judy, at that experience." These were, Cayce says, "seekers for the truth," also those "who counseled with the peoples—using the mathematical activities of the ages old, as well as the teachings of the Persians from the days of Zend and Og and Uhjltd*, bringing for those people a better interpretation of the astrological as well as the natural laws." It is interesting to note, in view of the importance Cayce ascribes to the study of astrology in the reckonings of these people, that the New English translation of the Bible, in the story of the birth of Jesus (the second chapter of Matthew) refers to these men as "astrologers" rather than "wise men." They are also frequently referred to as Magi, which was the name given to the learned, priestly class of ancient Persia.

Along with the continued study of astrological and numerological data and psychic experiences and revelations, both of the prophets of old and those of the Essenes and the associated groups of more recent times, there was, naturally, a continual expectation or hoping for further revelations to these dedicated people. And then there came some indication or awareness that an angel was to speak. Cayce does not specify the exact nature of this indication, but apparently something (possibly of an astrological nature) occurred which, according to records or traditions handed down from the "sages of old," had been observed to precede such an event. This was just at

* A period, according to Cayce, of high spiritual development. Zend, the son of Uhjltd, was the father of Zoroaster and was a former incarnation of the entity we know as Jesus.

the time when a husband for Mary was being chosen, and this brought to a focal point, says Cayce, the preparations of the maidens.

The choice of Mary as "she who was to be the mother of the promised one," according to Cayce, was made or announced by the angel when Mary was between the ages of twelve and thirteen, rather than being just at the time of or immediately before the conception, as seems to be implied by the Gospel of Luke. Luke also states that the angel appeared to Mary at Nazareth, but according to Cayce the choice was made "upon the temple steps." This was, of course, not the orthodox temple at Jerusalem but the temple at Carmel "where those who were consecrated worshiped."

Cayce gives an interesting sidelight concerning this temple which, he implies, had some bearing on its being the place where the choice took place. This group of Essenes, under the leadership of Judy, had studied the records, then still existent, of the Egyptian period when the activities in the Temple Beautiful and the Temple of Sacrifice had been a tremendous influence in the purification and spiritual direction of the people of that time. The activities of these temples, as interpreted from their studies, had been incorporated into the temple service at Carmel. "Hence," said Cayce, "it was in this consecrated place where the selection took place." He then proceeds to give a detailed account of the event:

"The temple steps, or those that led to the altar—these were called the temple steps. These were those upon which the sun shone as it arose of a morning when there were the first periods of the chosen maidens going to the altar for prayer, as well as for the burning of the incense.

"On this day, as they mounted the steps, all were bathed in the morning sun, which made a beautiful picture, clothing all as in purple and gold. As Mary reached the top step, then there were the thunder and lightning, and the angel led the way, taking the child by the hand

29

before the altar. This was the manner of choice; this was the showing of the way; for she led the others on this particular day."

After Mary was chosen as the channel for the entrance of the Messiah into the earth, she was separated from the others and kept in closer association with those who had the responsibility for the training and preparation. This latter part of her preparation apparently was over a period of approximately four years.

"Then," says Cayce, "when the days were come that the prophecy might be fulfilled that had been given by Isaiah, Malachi, Joel, and those of old, she, Mary, espoused to Joseph—a chosen vessel for the office among those of the priests of the sect or group who had separated and dedicated themselves in body, in mind, in spirit for this coming—became with child."

The "immaculate conception" has been a subject of violent argument from the time of the birth of Mary (if Cayce's account be accepted) even until the present time. The immaculate conception of Jesus is held as an important part of the doctrine of most, if not all, of the Christian churches, but the Catholic Church holds also to the doctrine of the "Immaculate Conception" of Mary.

This doctrine, according to the bull "Ineffabilis Deus" of Pope Pius IX in 1854, holds that Mary, "in the first instant of her conception was, by a singular grace and privilege of Almighty God in view of the merits of Jesus Christ the Saviour of the human race, preserved exempt from all stain of original sin." Whether or not this was meant to imply that Mary did not have a human father is debatable. The bull, as worded, could have meant simply that Mary had no inherent desire to sin. The term "immaculate conception" itself seems more significant. And the belief in the immaculate conception of Mary did not originate with this bull of Pius IX. The "Feast of the Immaculate Conception of the Blessed Virgin Mary" was observed as early as the seventh century, beginning in the East and spreading slowly through the West, where it met with a great deal of opposition. The belief was supported by the Franciscans from the thirteenth century, was affirmed as a pious opinion by the Council of Basel in 1439, and had become general in the Catholic Church before it was made a binding doctrine in 1854.

The Bible gives no information as to Mary's conception or parentage. Concerning the immaculate conception of Jesus, however, the Bible definitely speaks in the affirmative. It is true that the prophecy of Isaiah, generally accepted as being a prediction of the coming of the Christ, which reads in the King James version, "Behold, a virgin shall conceive and bear a son . . ." has been retranslated in other versions as "a young woman shall conceive . . ." But the Gospels are explicit on the subject. Matthew states unequivocally that "before they [Mary and Joseph] came together she was found with child of the Holy Ghost." And the question of Mary, as recorded in the Gospel of Luke, "How shall this be [the conception of a son, as the angel had predicted] seeing I know not a man?" indicates the same.

Still, many professing Christians cannot accept this belief. As remarked by Cayce, "This—the immaculate conception—is a stumbling stone to many worldly wise."

In other readings Cayce continues on this subject: ". . . they say, 'impossible!'—that it is not in compliance with natural law." It is a natural law, though, Cayce says, "as has been indicated by the projection of mind into matter, and thus making of itself as separation to become encased in matter as man did. Then, that there has been an encasement was a beginning. Then there must be an end when this must be or may be broken, and this began at that particular period. Not the only immaculate conception—this particular period with Ann, and then the Master as the son; but the only begotten of the Father in the flesh as a son of an immaculately conceived daughter. Neither Mary nor Jesus had a human father.

31

They were one soul, so far as the earth is concerned, for in the beginning Mary was the twin soul of the Master in the entrance into the earth."

Cayce is referring here to the concept of man's creation as a spiritual being and his subsequent involvement in materiality; this, given briefly and for the most part symbolically in Genesis, is explained in great detail in the Cayce readings.

It is given in Genesis that "God created man in His own image . . . Male and female created He them." Cayce's explanation of this, very briefly summarized, of course, is that the souls or spiritual beings, as Spirit itself, were neither male nor female but both—that is, that each contained within itself both male and female principles or both positive and negative polarities. The separation into male and female, he explained, and at the same time the involvement or entrapment in matter resulted from the desire to experience the animal activities which were a part of the earth plane. Thus materiality, limiting spiritual activity and ability of the soul, is closely related to the separation into male and female. The soul, in order to return to its original high estate and become a true son of the Father, must reverse this process, freeing itself from the bonds of materiality.

How may this be done?

Spirit, according to this concept given by Cayce, "pushed itself into matter" for its own gratification. "Spirit that uses matter," he says, "that uses every influence in the earth's environ for the glory of the Creative Forces, partakes of and is a part of the universal consciousness." This had been the experience, the activity of both Mary, the channel, and the entity entering as Jesus at this period.

Much of this entity's previous experience, the overcoming of materiality or "the world," is indicated by this information given by Cayce: First he was created, he says, as Adam, "brought into being from all there was in the earth, as an encasement for the soul of an entity, a part of the Creator, knowing separation in death." He was born then as Enoch, but so overcame the result of the law of disobedience as to merit the escaping of death. He was "made manifest as Melchizadek by desire alone . . . , brought into materialization as of itself, passing from materialization in the same manner." He entered into flesh again, by choice, "taking upon himself the burdens of the world," incarnating as Joseph, as Joshua and Jeshua, in each incarnation, through obedience to spiritual law, bringing the physical body, with its inherent desires, more into harmony with the spiritual. "Then," Cayce states, "there was perfected that period again in body when the other soul or portion of self was made manifest by the consecration of the mother; meeting self, then, by that same quickening power which had been made manifest in the beginning, or at first."

The immaculate conception is further defined by Cayce as "the physical and the mental so attuned to spirit as to be quickened by same. Hence, the spirit, the soul of the Master, then, brought into being through the accord of the Mother in materiality—that which ye know in the earth as conception."

Several different attempts to explain the immaculate conception were made by Cayce, in response to questions from different individuals. In all of these replies the "consecration of the mother" was emphasized, or "Love itself, which was manifest in the body of the Virgin."

"As the spirit was made manifest," one of these answers goes, "in the body purified by consecration of purpose in the lives manifested in the earth, so might the spirit—with the brooding of the body itself—bring to the organs of flesh a body through which the spirit may itself manifest in the earth."

There is not much in either sacred or profane history concerning the preparation of the mother for that channel through which immaculate conception might take place, and yet, Cayce says, "therein the world is shown that this must come to pass in the experience of those who would make themselves channels through which the Holy Spirit may manifest. Thus the world may know that He, God the Father, keeps His promises with the children of men."

Although a husband had been chosen for Mary, according to Cayce, even before the announcement by the angel that she was the chosen one, the marriage did not take place until some time after her conception of the Holy Child. The reason for this delay is not given—in fact Cayce says that the preparations for the wedding, when it finally took place, were made necessary by the fears produced among the Essenes by the "political turmoils with many of those peoples of the Holy family, or the house of the Lord." These turmoils were those brought about by the circumstances attending the birth of John, later called the Baptist.

The Gospel of Luke records the prophecy made by the angel Gabriel, as Zacharias, the priest, performed the service in the temple, concerning the coming of him who was to "turn the hearts of the fathers to the children," who was to "make ready a people prepared for the Lord;" and the promise was made to Zacharias that this forerunner should be born to his wife, Elizabeth, though she had previously been barren and "well stricken in years." And for his disbelief in the prophecy there came the dumbness that was to continue until the promise had been fulfilled.

Cayce adds a great deal more detail to the story, some facts both interesting and important to the understanding of the story of Jesus, John, and the attitude of the orthodox priesthood toward the Essenes and their tenets.

Zacharias, the son of Barachias, says Cayce, was a just man, a member of what might be called the orthodox priesthood. He was the priest who offered sacrifice for the month Nisan in the temple at Jerusalem, yet he lived in the hills of Galilee. For his wife, Elizabeth, the cousin of Mary, was an Essene, and for this reason Zacharias kept Elizabeth in the mountains and in the hills. The wisdom of this was made evident by subsequent events.

When the promise by the angel was fulfilled, and Elizabeth conceived, the Essenes began to consider the necessity of choosing the proper individual to act as the helper, or nurse, or director of this child who the angel had foretold would have such an important part in that for whch they themselves were preparing.

Then, when Elizabeth was "heavy with child," Mary visited her, and as is recorded in the Gospel of Luke, the child leapt in Elizabeth's womb when he heard Mary's voice. At this time, according to Cayce, the angel Gabriel again appeared, he who had made the choice of Mary upon the temple steps, and "she was made aware of the presence by being again in the presence of the messenger, or forerunner." Anna, the prophetess who had been active in the preparations for the maidens that had consecrated their lives for this expectancy, was acting as the waiting maid for Elizabeth, and she blessed them both, and "made those prophecies as to what would be the material experience of each in the earth."

When this experience was made known to those of the priesthood in Carmel, it was a reminder to many of what and how had been the choosing of Mary on the stair, and apparently the obvious relationship between the two events made them more aware of the necessity of choosing from among the dedicated women of their order one who would fill the needed office in relation to Elizabeth's child.

This may have presented quite a problem. Although Zacharias had married an Essene, it is not in any way indicated by Cayce that he, Zacharias, had been, up to this time, sufficiently in accord with them that he would have agreed to have the nurse for his child chosen by

35

the Essene leaders. The problem was solved, however, with the help of a woman named Sofa.

Sofa was a member of the Essenes, but she was "dedicated to service in the temple," not exactly as a caretaker. Her duties were to "touch up, or paint, or keep certain portions of the temple in order for the activities of the priest." This was apparently the temple at Jerusalem, for it seems that it was through these activities that she was acquainted with, or in association with Zacharias, for Cayce says, "Thus the entity [Sofa] appealed to Zacharias to use his period of preparation as the one to offer sacrifice as the time when there would be the choosing of the attendant or nurse for the babe." This was to be done by the method of divination or divine guidance "termed in the Cabala the moving of the symbol upon the vesture of the priest." It seems likely that this "symbol" was that referred to in the Old Testament as the Urim and Thummin. The following passages show the similarity:

"And thou shalt put in the breastplate of judgment the Urim and Thummin; and they shall be upon Aaron's heart when he goeth in before the Lord; and Aaron shall bear judgment of the children of Israel upon his heart before the Lord continually." (Ex. 28:30)

"And he [Joshua] shall stand before Eleazar the priest, who shall ask counsel for him after the judgment of Urim before the Lord." (Num. 27:21)

And from Deut. 33:8, a part of Moses' blessing of Israel before his death: "And of Levi he said, 'Let thy Thummin and thy Urim be with thy Holy one whom thou didst prove at Massah.'" Priests, according to the law of Moses, were to be of the tribe of Levi—thus the implication that the Urim and Thummin were to be used by all priests.

In what way the Urim and Thummin were consulted is not indicated in the Bible. Perhaps this mention by Cayce of the "movement of the symbol upon the vesture of the priest" furnishes a clue to this ancient mystery.

Possibly the movement of the symbol simply indicated a "yes" or "no" answer to a question and Sofa's name may have been suggested either by the Essene leaders or by Sofa herself. In any case, Sofa was chosen, and the method of choice, says Cayce, "prevented any of those confusions that might have arisen."

In due time the child was born, John, who was later called the Baptist. And when the birth was announced in the orthodox temple, and Zacharias related his experiences, his visions, proclaiming his belief in and adherence to the teachings of the Essenes, "he was slain, even with his hands upon the horns of the altar." This murder was apparently by, or at the instigation of "those of his own school." This must have referred to the Pharisees, since it was to the "Scribes and Pharisees" that Jesus spoke concerning the shedding of "the blood of Zacharias, son of Barachias, whom ye slew between the temple and the altar." (Matt. 23:35)

When Zacharias was slain, Elizabeth and the child "remained in safety," we are told, though there must have been the fear of danger to them, also, for they lived after that time "in the hill country of Judea," Cayce says, rather than in Galilee as previously. And Luke states that he (John) "was in the deserts until the day of his showing unto Israel." In view of these statements it is an interesting supposition that Elizabeth, with her son, may have sought refuge in the Essene community now believed to have existed at that time at Qumran.

The fears aroused by the slaying of Zacharias, Cayce says, made necessary the preparations for the wedding of Joseph and Mary, and the wedding was performed at Carmel. Why this wedding had been delayed until now is not explained. Possibly the Essenes had intended to make publicly known the fact that Mary's child was begotten not by a human father but by the Holy Ghost, but were now made aware that this would be extremely dangerous, and hence thought it important that she have a husband before the child was born in order that he not be considered "illegitimate."

It is not surprising that Joseph was much disturbed at finding Mary already with child at the time of the wedding. To begin with, the choice of Mary as his bride had not been his own, and he was not pleased with the choice. Though it was the custom in those periods in most Jewish families for the arrangements for marriage to be made by the parents of the contracting parties, in the case of Mary this had not been possible, since she and her mother, Ann, were not considered to belong to any, since Ann was unmarried. So the choice was made, not by the leaders of the sect, but by the priests as pointed out by divine forces. Thus was chosen Joseph, the son of Jacob, of the House of David.

When Joseph was first informed by Mathias and Judah, the leaders of the group at that time, of his selection as the one to whom Mary was to be espoused, this did not coincide at all with his own feelings. However, he accepted the situation when he was informed, "first in a dream, then by direct voice," that this was the divine will. When, however, after a period of some three or four years he went to claim her as his bride, and she was found to be with child, he was concerned as to what people would say, especially because of his advanced age as compared to that of the virgin when they were married; for he, Joseph was thirty-six at the time of the marriage, and Mary only sixteen. And even though he was assured by his brethren that this child of Mary's was of divine origin, it was only after the voice, the experience of the appearance of Gabriel, as recorded by Matthew, that he became reconciled to the idea of her pregnancy and accepted her as his wife.

Mary spent most of the time of her pregnancy, Cayce says, in the hills of Judea, a portion of the time with

Joseph in Nazareth. It is likely, from the record of Luke, that much of the time spent in the hill country was with Elizabeth, and it would seem probable that she lived with Joseph in Nazareth from the time of their marriage. It was from Nazareth that Mary, with Joseph, her husband, went out to be taxed, or to register for the tax when the decree went out from Caesar or his officials that the people should go, each to his own city for this purpose. Thus it was necessary, although the time was near that Mary should bring forth her child, that they make the long journey to Bethlehem of Judea.

CHAPTER THREE

THE BIRTH OF JESUS

The story of the birth of Jesus, the son of Mary, in Bethlehem of Judea, is probably the best known and best loved of all the narratives in the Bible. Each Christmas we hear or read the information given in the Gospels of Matthew and Luke concerning this event, and the beauty of the story is such that to many it never becomes tiring or monotonous. Yet now, through the information given by Cayce, we have a much broader, more detailed and comprehensive picture of the circumstances regarding this event.

The date was, according to Cayce's story, "not as counted from the Roman time, nor that declared to Moses by God, nor that same time which was in common usage in that land, but what would now represent January sixth." This will be recognized by many as being that date now celebrated as "Epiphany," meaning "manifestation" or "showing." It is also sometimes called "the twelfth day of Christmas." The event that Epiphany is supposed to commemorate varies in different churches, being variously considered to commemorate the baptism of Jesus, the visit of the wise men after his birth, and the miracle at Cana. In view of Cayce's giving this as the date of the birth of Jesus, it seems likely that, as some have said, the Church originally celebrated Christmas on this date, later beginning the celebration twelve days earlier as a matter of expediency, in order to relate to Christianity the celebration called Saturnalia then being held at that time.

The arrival of Mary and Joseph in Bethlehem was in the evening of that day, and the weather was cool, Cayce relates. There were great crowds of people traveling along the roads, for Bethlehem was only a "Sabbath-day's journey" from Jerusalem to which great throngs of people were traveling on their way from the hills of Judea. And those of the "house and lineage of David," as were both Mary and Joseph, were on their way to the city of David, called Bethlehem, for this, rather than the actual place of their birth, was considered "their own city," and each individual was required by the Roman law to be present in his "own city" for the polling. For representatives had been sent out by the Romans to judge the varied groups as to the amount of tax each was able to pay. "Both Joseph and Mary, being members of the sect called the Essenes," said Cayce, "were to be questioned and polled not only by those in political, but in religious authority in the city." Knowing the attitude of the religious authorities toward the Essenes, and considering the circumstances of Mary's pregnancy, this must have produced some apprehension.

Joseph and Mary were not alone in their journey, for they were accompanied by those of the household of Joseph, as well as many of his helpers—carpenter's helpers—and many of the varied groups or occupations from the fields about Nazareth, shepherds, husbandmen, and the like.

This group had been delayed on the journey by Mary's condition. When they approached the inn, therefore, in the evening, just at twilight, it was already filled with many of those people who had also journeyed there to be polled or register for the tax imposed by the Romans. And when they arrived, this "elderly man and the beautiful girl, his wife, heavy with child," they were met with the answer, "No room at the inn, especially for such an occasion!"

There was laughter and jeers from some of the rabble at the inn upon hearing this reply. "Disappointment was written on the face of Joseph," says Cayce, "and also on

41

the face of the innkeeper's daughter, as well as those of certain groups about the inn. Also there was consternation outside, among the Essenes who had heard that Joseph and Mary had arrived and were not given a room. They began to seek for some place, some shelter.

"For remember, many of those present were also of that questioned group. They had heard of the girl, that lovely wife of Joseph who had been chosen by the angel on the stair; they had heard of what had taken place in the hills where Elizabeth had gone, when she was visited by this girl, her cousin. Such stories were whispered from one to another.

"Thus many joined in the search for some place. Necessity demanded that some place be sought—quickly! Then it was found, under the hill, in the stable above which the shepherds were gathering their flocks into the fold."

While the story, as recorded in Luke, that "there was no room in the inn," is true as far as it goes, Cayce made clear that the usual interpretation of this statement is far from the true circumstance. And the impression generally held concerning the innkeeper who turned them away in spite of their desperate need is quite different from Cayce's description of the man and his activities.

The innkeeper, Apsafar, was of the Essenes, or in sympathy with them, though he was of Grecian as well as Jewish descent; and he apparently kept secret his religious convictions in order to act as a "go-between" between those in authority in the "religious influences in the Roman and Jewish faith." He was also involved with those "who were seeking to overcome those oppressions that were of a political as well as of a religious nature," not as a spy, but rather acting as a "counsellor." The political oppressions here referred to, of course, were the oppressions of the Jews by their Roman conquerors and those officials which would now be termed "collaborators." The religious oppressions were those caused by the intolerance of the Pharisees and Sadducees to other religious teachings than their own, such as those of the Essenes and "the teachings that were gradually being presented from the Grecians—Apsafar's own people."

One so closely associated with those in revolt against the established order of things, possibly even among the leaders of the revolutionaries, as would seem to be indicated by the word "counsellor," must have already been in a very dangerous position, without becoming involved in a situation that might call attention to him and his unorthodox activities. Still, having made a study of the Essenes, and knowing of those things that had been foretold by the teachers of those groups, he had made all the preparations in keeping with what had been foretold as possible.

"For," said Cayce, "it was well known to the innkeeper that which had been set by those high superiors or leaders, as to the care that must be given to those chosen ones as they wended their way to fulfill the needs or the requirements of an overlord demanding that all register for their contribution to an alien land."

It may have been through his daughter, Sarapha, that the innkeeper obtained much of his information concerning the activities, plans and expectations of the Essenes. For Sarapha, Cayce says, knew "somewhat of what was to come to pass through the meetings that were half forbidden by those in the Jewish law, and questioned by those in authority for the penal law." She was then "just a year younger than the little mother who came to the inn where Sarapha was then an aid to the parents," and as might be expected of any young girl with the curiosity natural to her age, such information brought about "a wonderment, a seeking to know." But Sarapha's interest was more, obviously, than that of a thoughtless, curious child. For "she felt," Cayce says, "the emotions of some great thing in the experience of the world about to come to pass," and she "requested that she might aid in the preparation of those quarters in which the mother-to-be and that father might come that were revered by all who were of that faith, that sect."

And Sarapha did aid, so that all was in readiness by the time that evening came. Then, "just before the sun set in all the glory of the Palestine hills," almost as though the voice of nature gave forth, "proclaiming the heralding of a new hope, a new birth to the earth, and the glorifying of man's hope in God—the spectre of His star in the evening sky brought awe and wonder to all that beheld. And Sarapha, being anxious, gazed with wondering awe at that experience, unusual to all, and wept with joy of those unfoldments within self, of the emotions that made for the expectancy of glory surpassing what had been told of all the glories of her peoples in the days of old. There she felt that a new light, a new vision, a new experience was being born in every atom of her being."

Then as the family waited for the coming of those glorious guests, there was the arrival of the general rabble, and the "discussions of those that journeyed to Jerusalem for the meetings, as well as to the centers for their taxing registration" brought doubt as to the safety or as to the advisability of having Mary and Joseph stay in the inn. For, because of the rabble, there was grave concern as to the "questionings that might arise from those in authority, both the Roman and the religious rulers of the land, as well as the various groups that were in their discussions making for the very things that would hinder or prevent those experiences that had been foretold." Therefore, the answer to Joseph and Mary, "No room in the Inn."

This answer was meant to imply to those not of the Essenes group that the newcomers were turned away. This was done for their own protection, rather than because there was no room. For Apsafar, the innkeeper too, Cayce says, "had seen a vision; he too had seen the star

44

in the east. He too had known of those experiences that must befall those that were making all the preparations possible under those existent conditions for Him that should come as a teacher, as a shepherd, as a savior."

It is easy to understand Sarapha's disappointment, when those looked for, hoped for visitors arrived, that they might not occupy those quarters in the inn that she had helped prepare, and also her concern as to the place that might be found for them. When it was made known to her that they were quartered in the stable, the cave under the hill, she was filled with the desire to be off to that place, to see what the experience might be. This was not possible immediately, of course, with the inn overflowing with guests, but as soon as her duties there were finished she started to the stable, which was very near. But as she walked into the open, accompanied by her mother, Sodaphe, "the brightness of His star," says Cayce, "came nearer and nearer. And she heard, even as the shepherds, 'Peace on earth, good will to men.' There came again that awe, that feeling of a new creation, of a new experience, as Sarapha, with only the closer attendance of the mother, hastened—while all the rabble, all the jeers of a world were stilled."

For "All were in awe," Cayce says, "as the brightness of His star appeared and shone. As the music of the spheres brought that joyful choir, 'Peace on earth,' all felt the vibrations and saw a great light—not only the shepherds above that stable, but those in the inn as well. To be sure, those experiences were later to be dispelled by the doubters, who told the people that they had been overcome with wine or what not." At the time, however, the star that the shepherds wondered at also caused awe and consternation to all those about the inn, and some who had made fun "were smitten with the conviction that the unkind things they had said must needs be readjusted in their relationships to things coming to pass."

45

Just at midnight, then, the Child was born, "who through the will and the life he manifested became the savior of the world," he through whom the promises made of old should be fulfilled—that promise made to Eve, that her seed should bruise the head of the evil one, that promise made in the wilderness of the arising again of another like unto Moses, and as given to David, that the promised one was not to depart from the channel of his descendants. Though man's concepts had fallen lower and lower, said Cayce, just when hope seemed gone—except to those few whose dedicated activities had made this event possible—the herald angels sang, that song that brought joy and awe to the shepherds, to Sarapha, and eventually to the world.

As Sarapha hastened to the quarters where the mother lay, "in all that awe of a new experience, and the light as from His star filled the place, she first beheld the Babe. That was the crowning experience, until the plea that she, too, might hold the glorious child in her arms." Then, as this became a reality, there were those feelings, those inner experiences which were to Sarapha as that which would never, could never be forgotten. It is little wonder that Cayce, in recognizing the feelings, the emotions of this girl, should have exclaimed at this point in the reading, "Oh that the world might know the beauty, the joy, the glory of the experiences of His life in their own hearts and minds and beings."

Sarapha was present when the shepherds came down from the hills to the stable where the child lay. These humble, lowly men, having heard the voice, the cry of "Glory to God in the highest!" having seen the light and experienced the choir of the angelic hosts that announced his advent, had come to see and to worship. Then, "on the morrow," Cayce says, "the wise men came with their laden beasts, or camels, with all their praise for those who had kept the faith in making preparation for, in keeping, helping, preserving those that were in need,

46

that were alone, yet God with them. And though that expressed was spoken in those tongues strange to Sarapha, their presence was such that she knew, she felt and experienced the reverence and awe as shown by all."

Sarapha was much impressed, according to Cayce's story, by the fact that these wise men, who came "as from the king," with all their glories, pouring at the feet of the child the gold and precious things of the earth, showed all the adoration that she had seen shown by the lowly shepherds. And yet these shepherds, so bewildered by those in power or in authority, with nothing to bring to him but love itself, were no less acceptable to him, she realized. For she saw, said Cayce, "that there was no respecter of persons in the face or heart of that Babe."

Cayce explains further who and what these wise men were. "In those days," he says, "there were men throughout the whole earth, the whole world, who looked for, sought for, the closer understanding. Hence, through the efforts of the students of the various phases of experiences of man in the earth, as may be literally interpreted from the first chapters of Genesis, ye find that those who subdued (not those that were ruled by, but those who subdued) the influences of that in the earth were considered, or were in the position of the wise, or the sages, or the ones that were holy in body and mind, in accord with purpose; and these were called then, wise men.

"We find, then, the wise men from Persia, and India, and Egypt, seekers for the truth about this event, through the application of those forces today termed 'psychic' coming to the place 'where the child was.' Yet they made their report concerning their search to the king."

It might be wondered, as Cayce pointed out, "as to why the wise men went to Herod, who was only second or third in authority, rather than to the Romans who were all authority in the land." It was, he explains, because of Judy, with whom there had been the discussions during the days of the preparation, "knowing that this

47

would arouse in the heart and mind of this debased ruler, that only sought for the aggrandizement of self, such reactions as to bring to him, this despot, turmoils with those then in authority." The reason for Herod's expected reaction and the fact that the Romans would not be likely to become perturbed is made more obvious by this statement of Cayce's: "There was not the proclamation made by the wise men, neither by Judy nor the Essenes, that this new king was to replace Rome. It was the fear of Herod that he was to replace the Jewish authority in the land."

Neither the wise men nor Judy, apparently, had the ability to predict the future in all cases. It is unlikely that they would have followed the course they did had they foreseen the actual results of this fear aroused in Herod.

While the Bible does not mention any Roman involvement in the wise men's search for the place of Jesus's birth, according to Cayce they were conducted to Bethlehem by "one of the Roman peoples stationed in Palestine that there might be the reckonings for the customs sought." This man, Puloas by name, had been largely responsible for tax collectors being chosen from the various faiths, the Jewish, Grecians, Helvetians and Egyptians, as well as the Romans. Since he was in the position of overseeing the establishing of these as collectors, he must have had some understanding of as well as sympathy for these various groups, yet his loyalty to Rome had been well proven when there had been turmoils from the uprising of the Jews that had rebelled, and he had been the commander of those that put down such raids. So "when the wise men came to seek out that answer, he was given the Roman charge that they be conducted to that place they sought. Then he became, even as they, a worshipper, a follower of those influences wrought in the minds and the souls and the hearts of men during those experiences."

The gifts brought by the wise men when they came to Bethlehem, the gold and frankincense and myrrh, represented in a metaphysical sense, said Cayce, the three phases of man's experience in materiality—gold, the material; frankincense, the ethereal; myrrh, the healing force —or body, mind and soul. These were the symbolic meanings. Also, "they were the encouragement needed for the mother and those who had nourished, who had cherished this event in the experience of mankind."

It is uncertain where the tradition arose that there were only three wise men who came seeking the newborn king. The Bible does not give the number, nor does Cayce, although the three gifts are mentioned in the Bible, and Cayce states also that the wise men came from three different countries.

Likewise, the number of the shepherds who saw the light and heard the angel's message is not given, either in the Bible or the Cayce readings. Cayce tells of three of them, however, Joel, Eucuo and Thaddeus, who were on the hills above the stable where the Child was born when they experienced that choir of the angelic hosts. One of them, Joel, was said to be elderly, a dreamer, a musician, impressed with the ability for song and poetry in the telling of those experiences. When they had seen the Child, and worshipped, they gave to the peoples thereabout the message of the angels. And those who were from the hills and who had come into the town for the tax registration heard the stories that the shepherds told, and returning to their own homes they carried the message thither, throughout Judea and Galilee.

Cayce reminds us of a point of great spiritual importance in a question he asks—and answers—concerning this event:

"When the hour approached when nature was to be fulfilled in the natural course in the experience of the Mother, and His star appeared, and the angels' choir, and the voices of those who gave the great message, who heard these, my children? Those who were seeking for the satisfying of their own personality? Rather to those who had given expression, 'No room in the inn,' (for no inn, no room, could contain that which was being given in a manifested form) and to those close to nature, to the hours of meditation and prayer. Only to those who sought could such a message come, or could there be heard the songs of the angels or that music of the spheres which sang, "Peace on earth, good will to men!"

So here we have, from the Cayce readings and the Bible, the information as to how he, the Light of the world, came into the world, though the world knew him not. He came unto his own, and unto those that received him came new life, new light, new hope, new joy, as to Sarapha, the wise men, the shepherds. And to us, also, these may come, if we heed the admonition given by Cayce in a reading for a group engaged in study for spiritual development:

"Let that love, that beauty which was the message to the shepherds be thine today: 'Unto *thee* is born . . .' Yea, unto thee, each one, is offered a knowledge, an understanding of the life of the Christ that will renew thy purpose—if ye will but sing that new song, 'Love one another'."

And to that same group, seeking to know more of the circumstances and conditions surrounding that which they called the first Christmas, he gave:

"Do not confuse yourselves. While to you it may seem to be the first Christmas, if it were the first then there would be a last, and you would not worship nor hold to that which passes. Time never was when there was not a Christ, and not a Christ mass.

"But in giving that interpretation of what this season means—the birth of Jesus who became the Christ—to this world: Much has been recorded respecting the circumstance by writers of the Gospel, especially by Luke; but no perfect concept may be gathered except by you as individuals seeking to experience what such an advent meant or means to your life as an individual.

"For the knowledge of a happening or condition, and

the wisdom which is presented by that happening are two different things. What you hear you may believe, but you will rarely act as if you believed it unless you have experienced and do experience that God so loved the world as to give His Son to enter into flesh, in order that flesh, man, might know there is an advocate with the Father.

"In your material experience you see that Life came out of nowhere to enter into materiality to become a living expression of those promptings of the heart. It has been the experience of that Christ Soul in its own varied spheres of consciousness to give you such an expression. That is the purpose for which He has entered—to give man a more perfect concept for the relationship between man and his Creator."

CHAPTER FOUR

THE EARLY YEARS

The holy family remained in Bethlehem until the time of purification was passed—twenty-nine days, according to Cayce, though this length of time differs somewhat from that given by Moses, as recorded in Leviticus, as the period of purification of women after childbirth. "The mother remained there, not deeming it best to leave, though all forms of assistance were offered; not leaving until there was the circumcision, and the presenting in the temple to the Magi, to Anna, to Simeon."

The presentation of the child in the temple and the presence there of Anna and Simeon is recorded in Luke, but there is no mention in the Bible that the wise men were among those to whom the child was presented in the temple. Bethlehem is the only place given at which they saw the infant Jesus. However, according to Cayce, "They came during the days of purification, but, to be sure, only after she [Mary] was purified were they presented to the child."

There is some question as to which, if any, of the women for whom Cayce gave life readings is the Anna who, according to Luke, prophesied concerning Jesus in the temple and blessed Mary and Joseph. There were several women of that name mentioned by Cayce in relationship to the Essenes and the period of the birth of Jesus, and there seems to have been sufficient similarity in the activities of several of these as to bring about some possible confusion. Two of these were said to have been prophetesses—as was the Anna mentioned in the Bible. Cayce definitely stated, however, that one of these, she who "sought through the mysteries of the sages to interpret time and place" of the coming of the Messiah, and who made the choice of the twelve maidens was "not the Anna in the temple." It is also unlikely that the other, the Anna who was the "waiting maid with Elizabeth and Mary when each was heavy with child" was the one who blessed Jesus in the temple; for the one in the temple was said by Luke to have been of extreme age. Also, after one reading in which an individual was told that she had been the "daughter of Elois, or the priestess that blessed the Holy One in the temple with Simeon," she asked whether this Elois and Anna were one and the same; and Cayce answered, "No, Anna was the older, or what would be termed the supervisor, or what would be termed by some as the lady superior of the group at the time."

There was also a woman whose name was given as Ananan, who was said by Cayce to have been "among the holy women in the temple," who "brought comfort and consolation, and proclaimed ever to the peoples of that period, 'Harken to the voice of Him who has called, If ye will be my people, I will be thy God! Turn ye to that way in which ye may bring again the sunshine of God's purpose among this people!' And as the entity prayed, as the entity lived that it might indeed see the day when that promise was fulfilled—thus when the Mother, Mary, presented the Babe in the temple, the entity blessed them, and saw that face!"

This seems very close to the account of the incident as given by Luke. Possibly the "Ananan" was a typographical error made in the transcript of the reading. However, it is also likely that many individuals not mentioned in the Bible were in the temple at the time of the presentation, especially some of the Essene group who would naturally wish to witness this religious ritual, similar to our present-day christening, and it is quite possible that the infant was blessed by more than one.

After the period of the presentation in the temple the family returned to Nazareth until the edict of Herod that made necessary the flight into Egypt. For this sojourn in Egypt was necessary, said Cayce, "owing to the conditions which arose from the visit of the wise men and their not returning to Herod to report, when the decrees were issued that there should be the destruction of the children of that age from six months to two years, especially in that region from Bethany to Nazareth."

How soon after the birth of Jesus this edict was given is not mentioned, either in the Bible or by Cayce. However, Herod could not have known immediately that the wise men would not return to report to him, and from the age of the children that were to be destroyed it is obvious that there must have been a period of at least six months before the edict was made.

The warning dream to Joseph may have come long before the edict. This is implied by the statement in Matthew, "When they [the wise men] had departed the angel of the Lord appeared to Joseph in a dream, saying, 'Arise, and take the young child and his mother and flee into Egypt . . .'" In seeming contradiction Cayce stated that there was the appearance of the angel, Michael, at the time "when the edict was given." This must have referred to the general period, however, rather than the exact time, since in another reading he says that it was "during those periods of the sojourn of the child in Egypt because of same. . . . Herod issued the edict for the destruction." Thus the warning was given and the journey begun before the issuing of the edict.

In any case, it was already known that this flight would be necessary, since Herod's reaction to the wise men's visit was anticipated, and plans and preparations for the journey had been made in advance. For, "soon after the birth," Cayce said, "there was the issuing of the orders first by Judy that there should be someone selected to be with the parents during their period of sojourn in Egypt."

The individual "selected or chosen by those of the

Brotherhood—sometimes called White Brotherhood in the present—as the handmaid or companion of Mary, Jesus, and Joseph in their flight into Egypt" was a young woman named Josie. Josie, the daughter of Shem and Mephibosheth, had been one of the companions of Mary during the days of preparation in the temple, or school, and had been close to Mary when her selection was indicated by the angel on the stair. Possibly this was a factor in the choice of Josie for this important position now.

"To many there might be questionings," Cayce says, "as to whether Mary was informed of the necessity for the flight, or merely Joseph—as Matthew records. However, as we find, they were of one mind, and the flight into Egypt—as is recorded—was the fulfilling of the prophecy. For it had been said, 'and my son shall be called from Egypt,' as given by Jeremiah as well as Isaiah."

When the time came for the journey to begin, "beasts" were obtained on which the mother and infant might ride. What these "beasts" were Cayce does not say, but since there was the need for being as inconspicuous as possible they would most likely have been the gentle, slow and plodding donkeys most frequently used by the common people of that time. This must surely have been, as Cayce says, a long weary journey for so young a mother with so young a child.

They were not abandoned at this point by the Essenes, left to the protection of God alone. Though to travel with a large group would have brought more danger by attracting more attention, Cayce says, "Do not understand that there were only Joseph, Mary, Josie and the child. For there were other groups that preceded and followed, that there might be the physical protection to that as had been considered by these groups of peoples as the fulfilling of the Promised One."

The journey to Egypt, though difficult, was accomplished without mishap or any event of great significance.

"The care and attention to the child and mother," says Cayce, "was greatly in the hands of Josie through that journey."

So began the period of the sojourn in Egypt and there was "the dwelling by the brooks or the portions where there were wells in the upper portion of the Egyptian land to which they fled, close to what was then Alexandria."

This was a period of great concern and distress for the people of the land of Palestine, not only for the Essenes in their concern for the safety of the Holy Child but also for all those parents of young children. For the decree issued by Herod "brought those periods," said Cayce, "that were best described as the cry of Rachel for her children that were being born into a period of opportunity—yet the destructive forces, by the very edict of this tyrant, made them as naught. For the edict was carried out, despite the attempts of the Romans to stay the destruction."

"A period of opportunity," indeed! For to many of that land, especially the Essenes, this was believed to be the time when great changes for the betterment of the people were to take place. And as is natural, many mothers and fathers thought, hoped, that their child might be the one to do some great thing, hold some important place in the new order of things. One such was a woman named Eunice, and her story as given by Cayce furnishes a good illustration of the attitude and the emotions that many parents must have experienced at that time.

Eunice lived in Galilee where at this time, Cayce says, there was less adherence to the orthodox Jewish doctrine or beliefs that had been established with the return of the people to the Palestine land from the Persian. Then as the ideals and tenents of the Essenes began to permeate more and more the religious activities of many of that land, Eunice's family became adherents to those teachings.

This family was a mixture of the Jewish and the Samaritan peoples, and there had been, in Eunice's early years, "the continued reports of happenings that were handed down as a part of the family records (for these were by word of mouth rather than from books)"— happenings that seemed miraculous, that seemed to indicate a special divine protection or "interference of Providence" in the preservation of both portions of the family.

For one branch, the Samaritans, were descendants of that remnant of the Israelites left in the land of Zebulun when the ten tribes had been carried away captive, and of the Babylonians who had been sent to colonize the land and with whom they had intermarried. And this group who were Eunice's ancestors had been preserved in the Promised Land, though they had maintained their adherence to the faith of their fathers through the changes which had been wrought.

The other portion of the family were descendants of the people of Judah who had been carried away by Nebuchadnezzar; and they had been returned to the land of promise by Cyrus, the Persian conqueror of Babylon, who had been recognized by the prophet Isaiah as "a shepherd" of the Lord (Isa. 44.28) and as His "annointed" king (Isa. 25.1).

It is little wonder, then, that "with the looking for the Savior, through the tenets of that new order" this "became something which, to Eunice induced the feeling . . . that to be sure, through the self must be the lineage that were to see and know and hear of this fulfilling of the promises in the day and age of her experience.

"Thus, with all such expectance, there was the betrothal; and then the birth of the son, that to Eunice must be one especially endowed with those privileges that were to mean and to bring such an awakening to the people."

This feeling, this conviction was increased or added to, Cayce indicated, through the associations with Elizabeth, the mother of John, and the friendships with Mary and Joseph, for their experience had been "a part of not only the conversation but the wonderments and the study of the entity [Eunice] through those periods of experience.

"And then there came the edict that robbed all the mothers of that particular portion of the land, through that which had been a part of the activities of one in the position to direct the activities through the counseling of the wise men, and their conversation and convocation with the king who made the edict.

"This brought into the experience of Eunice a spirit of hurt, of hate" for those who had, according to her understanding, betrayed those "whose sons were in those periods in which there was the expectancy and the desire for their fulfilling a long looked for promise." For it was asked whether or not sufficient consideration had been given for the safety of the other children of that land by those leaders of the Essenes who were said to have protected Mary and her son.

And through all that period, when Elizabeth was robbed of her mate "through the death even at the altar," through that period when she, too, was affected by "the very edicts of the king," Eunice's outlook began to change, and she attempted to understand why those who were supposed to be endued with powers and activities divine should have such things happen to them.

Help came to many of the distraught parents of that time and place, threatened with the loss of their children, from that which must have been an unexpected source. For many of the children Herod doomed to death were saved by Herod's own wife, Thesea, "through the preparing of means and ways for their being transposed or brought to other portions of the provinces."

The information given here concerning this individual, Thesea, comes from the Cayce readings alone. There is not, so far as this writer can find, any historical reference to Thesea as one of Herod's ten wives. It is possible, of course, that she was mentioned by some other name by Josephus, who gives a detailed historical account of this period, or that mention of this wife was purposely omitted. For it is interesting to note that Josephus also ignores the "massacre of the innocents" and the history of Christ. When Cayce was asked the reason for this he replied, "What was the purpose of Josephus' writing—for the Jews or for the Christians? This answers itself."

According to Cayce, Thesea, the daughter of a Jewish mother and a Roman father, was only fourteen years of age when she was married to Herod. She was chosen for her beauty and also for "the political influence that her family had with those in power as the priests." For her brother-in-law was the priest Caiaphas, who "made overtures to Herod in his proclaiming the closer relationships to the Roman rule." This, with the education or training she had received, fitted her in her "social as well as political affiliations" to be the wife of one in Herod's position. "Yet these were never close," said Cayce, and Thesea's personal feelings and religious interests were quite in conflict with those of her despotic husband.

She was well acquainted with many of those Essenes who lived in that portion of the land at the time; for she "was a seeker for not only the unusual but for the mystical powers proclaimed by many of that group through those periods of activity." She had reasoned with the Essenes, said Cayce; she had "conversed with the wise men who came with the new messages to the world." And having "sought a closer understanding of the wise men" she made "that pronouncement that He, Himself, then being announced had given [as Joshua], 'Others may do as they may, but as for me and my house, we will serve the living God.' "

Cayce here explained that "my house" did not have reference to those in the physical household, but that "thy house is indeed thy body—that is the temple of the living God. That is the whole house made to conform to the will, the way—'He that loves me keeps my commandments,' in body, in mind, in soul."

Certainly Thesea had no influence on those of her household in this respect, at least not upon her husband. Though his activities brought about "the determination to cry out—and she did," this only brought, later, "material or physical extinction," and influenced Herod not at all.

There were, even before the edict against the children, periods of persecutions that were, according to Cayce, "attempts of the companion [Herod] to court favor with the dictators or procurators who were in charge during those periods." These attempts apparently backfired, for, Cayce says, "This, as indicated by the Scripture, brought some disturbing conditions with those of the Roman rule, because of the changes that were probable, or that later came about, as to the emperors and their policies for handling those conditions and situations through the land.

"When there were the orders for the destruction of the individuals that their blood might be a portion of the sacrifice that was attempted, these brought abhorrence [to Thesea], and the turning away from the close associations with the activities of the companion at the period."

This slaying of the innocent children also brought to her, as to Eunice and undoubtedly to many of the people of that period, "great disturbance as to whys and wherefores of activities by or through the divine interference, or divine progress among men at the time. . . ."

"For," says Cayce, "there has not been the full concept as to the meaning of the blood as shed for the eternal sacrifice, or the law being of none effect in the law itself; that as individuals, in body, in mind, in spirit, *become* the law, it is then as void in *their* experience . . . for they *are* the law! And the law is love, the law is God, and the law *is* circumstance . . . as experienced in the activities there."

This period, to which so many had looked forward with so much hope and expectation, had become a time of sorrow and trouble and fear, and that not alone through the activities of Herod. "These were times when those of this troubled land experienced not only those periods when the law demanded that the children, the sons, were to be destroyed, but that even those who were consecrated might be abused the more by those activities of Roman power, that authority that had been given among that brotherhood as that from which man was to be freed."

Among those whose lives were much disturbed by the conditions of that time, who suffered from the persecutions, was the family of the innkeeper in whose stables Jesus had been born. "For oft was [Apsafar] questioned as to which way, as to what amounts, as to what were the activities of those men who had defied the authorities of Rome as well as of Herod the King at that experience."

This questioning, especially in view of Apsafar's previous activities, must have been frightening. And the nature or characteristics of his wife, as Cayce described them, must have increased the danger. For, Cayce says, while it was necessary "for the entity's position to be rather hidden, the entity in its purpose and its very activity was quite outspoken. Hence, with the visions, the experiences that came about during that particular period, she was awed . . . and then kept in that constant air of expectancy because of those periods through which there were the days of purification for the mother of the Son of God."

It must, indeed, have been very difficult to pretend to an ignorance of, or an indifference to, the happenings of such an exciting nature, still so fresh in her mind when the questionings came.

Sarapha, the innkeeper's daughter, had "sought to find, to keep in touch with the mother, the Child, and then when the edict went forth, indeed was the entity's heart rent with fear." For the moment when she held that Holy Child in her arms and pressed her lips to his brow had become a cherished memory, something to bring comfort through such trying times. Yet there was the "fear of the law, and the hatred that would naturally arise in the hearts of those that were persecuted."

There were days and weeks and months, Cayce says, when Sarapha wondered and wondered. Yet often, in the stillness of the evening, she "reviewed the happenings, and there was the seeking more and more as to what had become of His Star, His Light." And then she learned of the flight into Egypt by "the devious ways and manners in which there came the news through word of mouth."

All this was "in awe and quiet kept," yet these experiences became so much a part of her that, later, when she sat alone in the twilight, there was "almost again felt the music of the spheres, the singing of the morning stars," as the earth was quieted, and there entered "oft again that peace" that was only troubled by the cares of a workaday world.

The cruelty of Herod and the persecutions by his orders continued until his death—and even beyond. For, according to Cayce, the death of his young wife, Thesea, "was brought about by the decrees that were issued before the sarcoma germs brought death to Herod, himself." This order for her death was only "because of the aversion for her living beyond the period of Herod."

This is quite similar to the historical fact that, as he lay dying, he issued orders that after his death all the most important men of the kingdom should be executed so that there would be at least some tears upon his grave.

In the year 4 B.C. he died in loneliness and pain, this man called Herod "the Great," who indeed might have been truly great—had he not turned his back upon the ways of God.

CHAPTER FIVE

THE CHILDHOOD AND EDUCATION OF JESUS

We find nothing in the Bible or any historical source which gives a definite answer to the question of how long Jesus remained in Egypt. Matthew, the only gospel writer who tells of the sojourn there, states only that he "was there until the death of Herod." However, the fact, also given by Matthew, that Archelaus was reigning in Judea when the family "came into the land of Israel," indicates that some time had elapsed since the death of Herod; for it is known historically that Archelaus did not succeed to the throne of Judea immediately after the death of his father.

Herod, by his will, had divided the area over which he had ruled as puppet king into three parts, to be ruled over by his three sons. Archelaus was to reign over Idumea, Judea and Samaria, the central part of the country, Herod Antipas over Galilee and Perea, and Philip, the region beyond the Sea of Galilee. Caesar Augustus, however, did not ratify this will for some time. There were several pretenders to the throne, and the reign of terror begun by Herod's madness continued after his death in riots, tumults and civil war. Three thousand Jews were said to have been killed during one riot; two thousand to have been crucified following another uprising. In view of these conditions it would have been natural for Joseph and his family to have delayed their return to Israel for some time after Herod's death.

Apparently, according to Cayce, they did. In one reading he says, "The period of stay in Egypt was something over two and one-half years—until another ruler was in authority or power." In another he says, "There [Egypt] five years were spent, as ye term time . . ." These are not necessarily contradictory, as the longer period may have included the time spent in travel, the shorter time, the actual "stay" in and about Alexandria.

Alexandria was the greatest center of learning in all history, and was at that time especially a center of philosophical study; for the period of advancement of thought and learning called the "School of Philosophy" began there about 30 B.C. and continued for several centuries. The world-renowned library located there contained the literatures of many countries, including Egypt, India, Greece, Rome, and Asia Minor. It has been estimated that the library may have contained at one time as many as seven hundred thousand handwritten manuscripts.

Josie and the parents of Jesus were not indifferent to the opportunity for study during their stay in Alexandria. They studied those records which, according to Cayce, were "those same records from which the men of the East said and gave: 'By those records we have seen his star.' These pertained to what you call today astrological forecasts, as well as those records which had been compiled and gathered by all of those of that period pertaining to the coming of the Messiah. These had been part of the records of those in Carmel, in the early experiences, as of those given by Elijah, who was now the forerunner, who was now the cousin, who was (later) the baptist.

"All of these had been a part of the record, pertaining not only to the nature of the work of the parents, but as to their places of sojourn, and the very characteristics that would indicate these individuals and the character that would be a part of the experience to those coming in contact with the young child, as to how garments worn by the child would heal children. For the body, being perfect, radiated that which was health, life itself. Just as today individuals may radiate by their spiritual

Do you have room in your home for three wise men? They are Plato, Aristotle, and Marcus Aurelius ... three of the wisest, wittiest, most stimulating minds that ever-lived.

They still live ... in the Five Great Dialogues of Plato, the Meditations of Marcus Aurelius, and Aristotle's On Man in the Universe.

All three books (regularly $11.67) can be yours for only $1.00 as your introduction to the Classics Club.

The Classics Club is quite un-like any other book club.

The Club does not offer best sellers that come and go. Instead, it offers its members a chance to stay

LET THESE 3 WISE MEN INTO YOUR HOME.
LATER, YOU MIGHT LIKE TO INVITE THEIR FRIENDS.

ENJOY THE COMPANY OF THREE OF THE WISEST MEN WHO EVER LIVED

(Continued from other side)

The selections themselves are remarkable values. They are carefully printed on expensive paper stock. They are hard-bound in matched sand-colored buckram, worked and stamped in crimson, black, and genuine gold. And through direct-to-the public distribution, we are able to offer our members these deluxe editions for only $3.89 each, plus shipping.

Interested? We will send you the first three selections, Plato, Aristotle and Marcus Aurelius—all three

selves health, life, that vibration which is destructive to disease in any form in bodies."

Studying this sort of thing, Mary and Josie speculated as to whether or when those predictions concerning these unusual powers of the child would be proven true.

When the journey back to the Promised Land was begun, Cayce says, Jesus was "in every manner a normal, developed body, ready for those activities of children of that particular period." He explains, however, that this should not be interpreted in the light of childhood in our own land at the present time, but rather of the Oriental. For the customs which had influenced the activities of Jesus during these early years of his life were those of Egypt as well as of Galilee.

Through that period of the return from Alexandria there were those incidents, the stories of which "have come down as legends, even of those people in some portions of Egypt and of Arabia, as to how there were the unusual happenings—indicating not only the divinity of the child, but that purpose later recorded, 'And she kept all of these and pondered them in her heart.' "

Although this statement in the Bible that is quoted here refers to a later incident, Cayce explains that it also applies to Mary's comparison of these experiences with the records that she, as well as Josie, had seen. "These records, of course," he says, "were destroyed at a much later period."

Matthew records that when Joseph came into the land of Israel with the young child and his mother, and learned that Archelaus was ruling in Judea, he was afraid to go there, but chose instead to go into Galilee.

The history of this time and place makes this very understandable. The people of Judea, though they had had reason to rejoice at the end of Herod's reign, found themselves no better off under the rule of Archelaus. Archelaus had angered the people, first by refusing their requests for remission of taxes and punishment of Herod's advisors after having asked them what he could do to please them; later by a marriage which they considered contrary to the Jewish religious law; and finally by taxing them heavily to rebuild the palace at Jericho in a magnificent manner and to build a city to be called by his name. When violence broke out as a result of the intense anger of the people, Archelaus met this in a heavy-handed manner, with police rule and repression.

How much of this had occurred at the time Jesus's family returned to the Holy Land is not known, but this situation was undoubtedly that of which Joseph was "warned of God in a dream," as Matthew reports. By going into Galilee, a quieter and more secure domain at the time, the family became subject to Herod Antipas, rather than Archelaus.

Cayce gives an additional reason for the return to Galilee. "The return was made," he said, "to Capernaum, not Nazareth, not only for political reasons, owing to the death of Herod and the division that had been made with the kingdom" after his death, but also that "there might be the ministry or teaching that was to be a part of the activity of the Brotherhood, supervised by Judy as among the leaders of the Essenes at that particular period.

"Hence, much of the earlier education of Jesus, the early activities, were those prompted or directed by that leader, but were administered by, or in the closer associations by Josie. Though, from the idea of the Brotherhood, the activities of Josie were no longer necessitated she preferred to remain, and did remain" as long as Jesus was in the home. She "was active in all educational activities, as well as in the care of the body, and the attending to the household duties with every developing child."

Jesus's studies during this early period, according to Cayce, were those "in keeping with the tenets of the Brotherhood, as well as that training in the law, which was the Jewish or Mosaic law in that period." The interpretation of the law was, of course, in accordance with the activities and beliefs of the Essenes, and that "outlined for the parents and the companions of the developing body."

The Bible gives us no information at all concerning this period of the life of Jesus, from the time of the return to Palestine until he was twelve years old. What he was like as a child has been a subject of almost endless conjecture and wondering. Was he, as in many fictional stories, and as some have claimed, able to perform miracles, and was he clairvoyant and clairaudient? Cayce gives us an answer.

"Remember and keep in mind—he was normal," Cayce says. "He developed normally. Those about him saw those characteristics that may be anyone's who wholly put the trust in God." Though "the apparel brought more and more the influence which today would be called a lucky charm," this was "not as a consciousness. This began [the consciousness of his powers and abilities] with the ministry, from that period when he sought the activities from the entrance into the temple and disputing or conversing with the rabbis at the age of twelve. Thus the seeking for the study through the associations with the teachers at that period."

Luke's account of this incident is well known—how the young boy, Jesus, stayed behind in Jerusalem after the Passover feast, and was not missed by his parents until they had gone a day's journey towards home. "It was thought by Joseph and Mary," Cayce says, "that it was in the care of Josie that he had stayed, when he was missed, in those periods when there was the returning to find him in the temple." For Josie had been "among those who went with Mary and Joseph when they went to Jerusalem at the time." She returned with them to the city, and heard him questioning the learned men, and rejoiced; for she was among the few who understood when he said, "Knew ye not that I must be about my Father's business?"

67

Another of those who were present and to whom this occasion brought joy and an understanding of his meaning was Sarapha who had once, on the night of his birth, held this child in her arms.

In the days and months and years that followed the return of Jesus to the Holy Land, Cayce said, Sarapha had eventually become "closer to those in Bethany, and those upon Mount Olive. For there she took up her abode, upon the edge of Olivet, on the road that led to the great city. And there word was sought again of what had become of that glorious, that marvelous experience which to Sarapha became more and more a burning experience in the heart. Yet when the persecutions came, and the influence more and more of the Romans, and more and more of the sects and the activities of the Sadducees that persecuted, especially, those groups to which Sarapha had belonged, and in which she found so much help, so much wonderment, then doubt and fears arose."

Sarapha's father had met his death through those persecutions, after which Sarapha "prepared or kept an inn herself, upon the Mount of Olives, nigh unto Bethany, on the road from Jerusalem to Gizeh." To be left alone without father or husband in those perilous times could have been a frightening thing for a woman, but Sarapha's "doubts and fears" were apparently not for her own personal safety, but for that upon which she had based her hopes for her people, and for the fulfillment of her glorious vision—the significance of the coming of the child whose birth had brought such a wonderful experience.

"For apparently," says Cayce, "from the words that were heard, the child had become only as another of those that were of the peoples—yet was it for all the peoples." For as other children came, and as other experiences were brought about, the memories of the happenings at his birth seemed to have faded in the minds of many. Sarapha, too, apparently had some doubts as to whether her interpretation of the events of his birth, and that which she had experienced within herself, was correct, for, Cayce says, "not until those days in which, as a child, he went again with his parents and those of the great company to again register did Sarapha realize and know the truth of what had been experienced.

"For at the time or period when the Passover feast was demanded to be kept by all of the children of Israel, then Sarapha sought again that child, that young man, that glorious child that questioned the doctors. And she kept close that she too might hear."

Surely her doubts and fears as to the fulfilling of the prophecies were laid to rest when she heard the expression of his wisdom and understanding, and his reply to his mother, "I must be about my father's business," even as doubts and fears as to the purposes of God in any troubled time may be quieted by the following of this example in the lives of men.

Sarapha, though "comely in person," and having been sought after as a wife, had "put away all thoughts of association or union with men—even though she was "beset and disturbed" by the conditions under which it was necessary to live in those unsettled times. For she, Sarapha, "became what may be said to be the first to dedicate her mind, her body, her being, her purpose to a child."

It has been generally assumed, often even stated by writers and teachers of religion or theology, that Jesus was uneducated. Yet surely many must have wondered why, if this were true, he was called Rabbi and Master even by those who were not his disciples, or why when he went into the synagogue he was given the scroll of Isaiah to read to the congregation. It would not seem customary in relation to the uneducated carpenter that Jesus is usually thought to have been.

In our own time a definite course of study, a "higher education," must be completed before a man is designated a rabbi by those of the Jewish faith. All available evidence indicates that this was true, also, in the time of Jesus, that the word was a "title for those distinguished for learning, authoritative teachers of the Law," as is a dictionary definition.

Jesus was, indeed, according to Cayce, "distinguished for learning," an "authoritative teacher of the Law," and also a Master of the teachings of the East. He had already attained to a thorough knowledge of the Jewish law through his studies at home before his twelfth year. "After the period of presentation again at the temple, when there were those questionings among the groups of the leaders," Cayce says, Jesus left the household of Joseph and Mary, and was in the care and ministry of the priests and leaders of the Brotherhood.

From his twelfth to his fifteenth or sixteenth year he was taught the prophecies by Judy in her home at Carmel. Then began his education abroad. He was sent first again into Egypt for only a short period, then into India for three years, then into that later called Persia—one year in travel and in Persia. From Persia he was called to Judea at the death of Joseph, then went into Egypt for the completion of his preparation as a teacher.

"In the studies that were a portion of the preparation," Cayce said, "these included first those that were the foundations of that given as law. Hence from law in the Great Initiate must come love, mercy, peace, that there may be the fulfilling wholly of that purpose to which he was called." The teachings he received in India were of "those cleansings of the body as related to preparation for strength in the physical as well as the mental man. In the travels and in Persia, the union of forces as related to those teachings of Zu and Ra. In Egypt, that which had been the basis of all the teachings in the temple, and the after-actions of the crucifying of self in relationships to ideals that made for the abilities of carrying on that called to be done. Hence, in all the ways of the teachers was Jesus trained." In all his studies, Cayce said, he was registered under the name of Jeshua. This name and its variant, Joshua, of which the Greek form is Jesus, are contractions of Jehoshua, meaning Help of Jehovah, or Savior.

John, the messenger, the forerunner, was with Jesus during a portion of the period spent in Egypt, though John was in one class, Jesus in another. For while Jesus was in India, John, at the age of seventeen, had gone into Egypt for the dedication and preparation there.

Jesus and John were in Heliopolis "for the periods of attaining to the priesthood, or the taking of examinations, passing the tests there. These, as they have been since their establishing, were tests through which one attained to that place of being accepted or rejected by the influences of the mystics, as well as of the various groups or schools in other lands. For . . . the unifying of the teachings of many lands was brought together in Egypt, for that was the center from which there was to be the radial activity of influence in the earth, as indicated by the first establishing of those tests, or the recording of time as it has been, was, and is to be, until the new cycle is begun."

The ancient city of Heliopolis, according to the New Standard Encyclopedia, was a center of learning long before the establishment of Alexandria. It was especially notable for its schools of astronomy and philosophy, but it declined after the founding of Alexandria. It was located about six miles northeast of modern Cairo, not far from the Great Pyramid of Gizeh.

The Great Pyramid was built, Cayce says, "to be the Hall of the Initiates of that sometimes referred to as the White Brotherhood. In that same pyramid did the Great Initiate, the Master, take those last of the Brotherhood degrees with John, the forerunner of him at that place."

A portion of the initiation there—referred to in the Gospel as three days and nights in the tomb—"is a part of the passage through that to which each soul is to attain in its development." For each soul, each individual as an initiate must pass through those same stages in its development as those through which the earth itself, or the peoples of the earth as a whole must pass—and this is shown or indicated in the passage through the pyramid, ending in the chamber in which stands an empty tomb. "All changes that came in the religious thought in the world are shown there, in the variations in which the passage through same is reached, from the base to the top —or to the open tomb *and* the top. These are signified by both the layer and the color in what direction the turn is made."

Through these stages the Master passed in his initiation, coming at last to that of the overcoming of death, or the breaking of the tomb, the releasing of the soul from its bondage to the material world and death—thus the empty tomb.

"And there, as the initiate, he went out for the passing through the initiation by fulfilling that as indicated in the baptism in the Jordan, as he passed from that activity into the wilderness to meet that which had been his undoing in the beginning."

CHAPTER SIX

THE MINISTRY OF JESUS

Political changes had been coming about in the land of Palestine during the period of Jesus' childhood and education. Although the tetrarch, Herod Antipas, still ruled in Galilee, Archelaus had proven an unsatisfactory ruler and had been exiled about six or eight years after his rule in Judea began.

The territory over which Archelaus had ruled had been made into a Roman province, administered by procurators. These were not of the aristocracy, but of the "equestrian order," so called because this order or rank derived from the Roman cavalry. Thus Cayce refers to this administration as "the establishing of the proletariat over a portion" of the country. These governors, or procurators, however, had a large degree of kingly powers, such as full powers of criminal justice. During the ministry of Jesus, Pontius Pilate, the fifth of the procurators of Judea, was in power there.

During the rule of Herod the Great over the whole of the land of Palestine, or "during those cross-purposed edicts of the Roman ruler and Herod," Cayce says, the meetings of the adherents to the Essene beliefs had necessarily been kept secret, but after the death of Herod, when Herod Antipas came into power in Galilee, "more consideration was brought or given to those who called their meetings in those various manners." Also it seems that, since the Roman authorities did not ordinarily interfere with the religious activities of the people of their subject provinces, the Essenes in Judea had, for a time, more freedom of movement or activity. Thus, after the return of John from Egypt, though he was then, according to

Cayce, the head of the Essenes, or that known as the White Brotherhood, his purposes and activities were openly proclaimed.

In those days just before the ministry of the Master began, John, as we are told in the Gospels, was preaching in the wilderness, and baptizing in the Jordan. As the lineal descendant of a priest, of the temple service, he was entitled to inherit this position of wealth, glory and prominence, yet his way of life was quite different from that which he might have chosen. For, said Cayce, "he had, through the prayers, the activities of those consecrated souls, those among the Essenes, become one capable in the flesh of renouncing the priesthood and to become an outcast, that there might be made known what had been proclaimed by those of old, that he should be as the voice of one crying in the wilderness, 'Prepare ye the way, for the day of the Lord is at hand.' "

Cayce tells how Andrew, "the fisherman on the Sea of Galilee," became, through the message of John, the first of the followers of "the Nazarene, the Gift to the world":

"In the days when John began to teach in the wilderness, Andrew became first an adherent and a disciple of that teacher, and remained close as an aide from first conviction until the appearance of Jesus to become the disciple of Andrew's master. When pointed out by John as the one that should be the greater, and increase as he decreased, Andrew then followed the new leader into the wilderness, and was close with him during the temptation, as is recorded in Matthew." For "he was tempted in all ways like as we are: in that of self-indulgence, of self-gratification, of self-glorification—yet without sin."

Then Jesus, followed by Andrew, returned to the Sea of Galilee. This might not be called a sea in most portions of the world today; but the Hebrews applied this term to lakes of moderate size, and this sea, or lake, was about thirteen miles long and six in width. This is the lake also spoken of at times as the Lake of Gennesaret, the Sea of Tiberias, and the Sea of Cineroth.

No fewer than nine cities stood on the shore of the lake, one of the larger of these being Capernaum, where the dwelling of the Master's family was. A few miles distant, near to that place where the Jordan enters the lake at its northern end, was the town of Bethsaida, where Andrew then lived.

Andrew, according to Cayce, was "the second brother in a family of four, and in the early childhood, one willful in many ways"; yet in manhood he was referred to by Cayce as "staid," in contrast to Peter, his brother, whom Cayce described as "boisterous." A mutual friend was said to have "argued with Peter and reasoned with Andrew," which indicates something of the difference in the nature of the two brothers.

As soon as Jesus and his new disciple had returned to the sea shore, then Andrew "sought out the brother, telling of those ideas, ideals, as was propounded by him who had been pointed out, and he became the close disciple then of the Teacher and Master."

The first miracle of Jesus recorded in the Gospels is the changing of water into wine at the wedding in Cana. Information concerning the circumstances of this occasion comes to us from several of the Cayce readings.

"Soon after the return of the Master from the Jordan," said Cayce, "and his dwelling by the sea, his conversation with Peter—after Andrew had told Peter of the happenings at the Jordan, there was the wedding at Cana of Galilee.

"The girl was a relative of those close to the mother of Jesus, who prepared the wedding feast, as was the custom in that period, and is yet among those of the Jewish faith who adhere to the traditions as well as the customs of those people chosen as the channel because of their purpose with God." She, the bride, "was a daughter of the cousin of Mary, a daughter of a younger sister of

Elizabeth, whose name was also Mary. She was the one spoken of as 'the other Mary,' and not as some have supposed."

Mary, "the other Mary," Cayce says, was among the household of Zebedee as an aid to Zebedee's wife and James and John and their sister Naomi, the younger of Zebedee's children, were in their early years Mary's charges or cares. John, the younger of the family as well as the younger of those chosen by the Master, that one called "the beloved," was an especial favorite of Mary.

"The groom, in the name of Roael, was among the sons of Zebedee, being an older brother of James and John, who later became the close friends and closer followers of Jesus."

"The families of Mary were present, as well as those of the groom. The Master, returning with those who were hangers-on, naturally sought to speak with his mother. Learning of this happening, he too, with his followers, was bid to remain at the feast.

"The customs required that there be a feast which was composed of the roasted lamb with the herbs; the breads that had been prepared in the special ways which were the custom and tradition of those who followed close to the faith of Moses' law, Moses' custom, Moses' ordinances.

"Much wine was part of the custom. The day was what ye would call June third, and there were plenty of flowers and things of the field, yet only a part of those things needed. For the custom called for more of the meats prepared with certain herbs, and wines.

"The day had been fine; the evening was fair; the moon was full. This, then, brought the activities with the imbibing more and more of wine, more hilarity, and the dance—which was in the form of the circles that were a part of the customs, not only of that land, but that are in your own land now and then being revived.

"With those activities as indicated, the wine ran low.

76

Remember, the sons of Zebedee were of the upper class, as would be termed, not the poorer ones. Thence the reason why Mary served or prepared for her relative at the feast.

"From those happenings that had been a portion of her experience upon their return from Egypt—as to how the increase had come in the food, when they had been turned aside as they journeyed back towards the Promised Land—Mary felt, knew, was convinced within herself that here again there might be such an experience, with her son returning as a man starting upon his mission.

"For what was the pronouncement to the mother when Gabriel spoke to her? What was the happening with Elizabeth when the mother spoke to her? This might be called a first period of test. For had he not, just ten days ago, sent Satan away, and received his ministry from the angels? This had come to be known as hearsay."

Hence, says Cayce, there was the natural questioning of the "mother-love" for his purposes. For this son, strange in many ways, had chosen, by dwelling in the wilderness for the forty days and then returning to the lowly people, the fishermen about this country, a way that seemed strange for one who had mastered the teachings of the East. Therefore, a question was implied when Mary told Jesus "They have no wine."

And though he said, "My time is not yet come," yet Jesus gave the commands whereby this miracle came to pass, when the water was turned into wine. Or, as expressed by Cayce, Jesus "caused the wine to blush— water saw its master, blushed and became wine, even by activity."

"Remember," he admonished, "only when it was poured out would it become wine. Had it remained still, no wine would have filled those conditions where embarrassment was being brought even to the friend . . ."

This, the first record of the miracles of the Master, is one of the few instances, as Cayce comments, where miracles were ever performed among his own people, his own kindred.

The family of Zebedee, whose son, Roael, was the bridegroom at that wedding in Cana, "were not of the rabble," Cayce says, though neither were they "of the political, or of great spiritual influences or forces among the associates of the group." Zebedee, however, was "influential with those in Roman or Jewish power at the period, "for he was "among the wealthy" and was closely associated with those in authority."

While both Zebedee and his wife Mary "were of the Jewish faith, or the Hebraic faith, they were in that position, socially, which was above that of the ordinary individuals. For these, Mary and Zebedee, were one of the house of Judah, the other of the house or lineage of Levi, and closely associated with those of the priesthood, though "by and through the associations of Zebedee there were the contacts with the Essenes and those groups that held rather to a more universality of application of the tenets and teachings of the peoples during that period."

Owing to the customs of the group to which Zebedee belonged (that is, the Essenes) "this necessitated the choosing of a following or vocation somewhat in keeping with the forefathers," and Zebedee was engaged, as were his sons, in the fleets, or fishing, upon the Sea of Galilee. Yet the location of the home or dwelling was in Judea, "outside of Jerusalem, nigh unto Bethany." Also, "the activities of Zebedee required that the purposes and aims be rather carried on by agents." Therefore, Zebedee "was given to the obtaining and leasing of privileges to others," or was, "in the parlance of the present, in the fishing business as a wholesaler, rather than being in active service himself." This, however, Cayce says, was only a small part of Zebedee's activities.

In these surroundings, then, the home life of Zebedee's younger children the influence upon them, had been out of the ordinary, even in that period of experience. For

Mary, the mother, was of the family of the priesthood that had been renounced by the cousin, John. Zebedee had been at first in the Essene temple at Carmel but had "had a fuss with Judy," and was then closer in the one in Jerusalem, "though not strictly orthodox, as indicated by being both a landowner and a fisherman." Roael, the older brother, was also active among the Essenes. So the children were "pulled, as it were, between the teachings or the training of the mother and the activities of the father and brother; yet had associations in the Roman activities, as well as a position in the Jewish faith or Jewish activity."

The children were "educated in the schools of those that were the teachers from Carmel, yet associated with those activities of the people about the temple, and those who dedicated themselves to the service that was to bring those activities which to the world today find themselves exemplified in many ways; in one, the sisters of the orders of that known as the Catholic Church in the present; in the other, the orthodox activities of the sisters of mercy among certain Jewish sects.

"These, then may give the conditions, the activity," in which Naomi and James and John found themselves in their early teen years—"pulled between whether the holy activities of the Essenes or the dedicating of selves to the faith of the fathers."

When there first began those activities among John's teachings they joined then with those of the Essene group—not only the brothers, but also Naomi, who was in age between James and John. For John, he who was later called the Baptist, as the head of the Essenes first taught that the women who chose might dedicate their lives to a specific service.

"Hence, not only the brothers, but those employed by the brothers, Peter, Andrew, and Judas (not Iscariot) joined in the activities. These were of the fisherfolk who aided in the establishing the teachings in and among the people that held to both the old and the new environs."

Cayce refers to that incident "as indicated or given [in the Gospel] that as he [Jesus] passed by he saw James and John with their father Zebedee mending their nets. "Rather," he says, "were the brothers and the father supervising and reasoning with the employees as to their activities." This was that incident when he called to them to come and be "fishers of men."

At first, says Cayce, Zebedee "was averse to the interest of James and John" when they came under that influence. But "with the better acquaintance" with the activities of the Master, Zebedee "grew into that attitude [of being] a greater advocate of the 'all out' administration of self and self's abilities, of self's physical, mental and material abilities, for the welfare of those in spiritual truth. As was manifested, as was maintained, a stickler for a set rule of formality, yet that also of the perfect, or more perfect, understanding of the true meaning of those abilities for one to be tolerant with others."

When the first Sabbath had come following Jesus's return to Capernaum to dwell with those of his own people, he went into the synagogue of that city, and was shown the deference due a rabbi in Israel—until the tenor of his teachings and the authority with which he spoke started to evoke astonishment and dismay.

The report of this important incident, which marks the real beginning of Jesus' teaching among his own people, is given by Luke: How Jesus, having read the prophecy concerning the ministry of the annointed one from the book of Isaiah, said to the congregation, "This day is this scripture fulfilled in your ears." Luke's account, however, differs from that which Cayce gives, as to the setting of the story, for Luke says this occurred "in Nazareth, where he had been brought up," and that afterward he "came down to Capernaum . . . and taught them on the sabbath days. And they were astonished at his doctrine, for his word was with power." According to Cayce, this all occurred in Capernaum, rather than being separate incidents in separate places.

It should be borne in mind that, according to Cayce, Capernaum was the city "where he had been brought up," though the fact that he was called a Nazarene could easily have caused some confusion on this point. Therefore, this part of Luke's record, which by his own statement was only hearsay, would be a very natural mistake, if he is the one in error on this minor point.

According to Cayce, Ruth, the daughter of Mary and Joseph, was in the synagogue when Jesus first spoke there, and heard "his first utterances as to the prophecies of Isaiah, Jeremiah, and the teachings of the lesser prophets, and as to how they applied in the experiences of that day."

Ruth, the sister of Jesus, is not mentioned by name in the Bible. Whether the brothers and sisters mentioned in Matthew 13 and Mark 6 were actually blood brothers and sisters, or only cousins or other relatives, is a disputed question, since many believe that Mary remained a virgin throughout her life. However, several references in the Epistles of Paul seem, to many scholars, to indicate that James and Judas definitely were not brothers of the Lord, though he does not mention the other two, Joses and Simon, named as among his brothers by Matthew and Mark.

According to Cayce, these two, James and Jude (or Judas) were children of Mary and Joseph, as was also Ruth. Mary remained a virgin, he says, only "until Jesus went to be taught by others." Only then "did the normal or natural associations come about. These associations began then as normal experiences."

"Soon after that recorded in Writ of the journey to the city for that period of the Passover teachings," Cayce says, "we find that James was born. In the next year, when there had been by the Wise Men of the East the beginnings of the teachings of Jesus, these activities

81

brought about a change in the material or financial status of the family." In that year, Ruth, the daughter, "was born in the city of Capernaum and surrounded with the activities that befitted the peoples of that period, that day." Jude, the youngest of Mary's children, was born within the next few years.

After that meeting in the synagogue "where a tumult was raised owing to the utterances of that new teacher," Ruth returned home "in haste to acquaint the mother with the sayings of that teacher, the brother of whom so much had been asked, by whom so much had been said, but so little understood by Ruth."

That Ruth should be both excited at her brother's teachings and concerned at the resulting violent anger of his hearers is understandable. Cayce's information concerning the circumstances in which she grew up, and especially the awe and mystery she had felt concerning Jesus, makes her emotional turmoil even more understandable.

"There was awe in the minds of the peoples," Cayce said, "as to what had taken place at the birth of the mother's or Mary's first son. Hence, the daughter, Ruth, was rather in awe of the suggestions, the intimations that surrounded that experience, and questioned the mother concerning same."

Ruth was still a young child when "the death of Joseph brought that brother, Jesus, home," yet not too young to be greatly affected by this association and the attitudes of those around her, "those activities . . . concerning that unknown, that strange kinsman whom the people held in awe, yet said many unkind things about him."

Then there was "the departure of that brother into Egypt for the final initiations or teachings with John— another kinsman who had been spoken of and held in awe." It is no wonder that in Ruth's girlhood years "such ponderings brought a great many disturbing influences" to her.

The association throughout her early years with Josie, who had been acquainted with all those things predicted concerning her oldest brother, must have contributed to Ruth's wonder—for Josie had "remained with the mother, Mary, through those experiences, ministering to her when the other children came," and when Joseph died, "closed his eyes and laid him to rest," and was active "in the preservation or keeping of the family intact" after his death.

When the period had come for the education of Ruth, she "was educated not only in the best of the land, but in other lands," in both Greece and Rome. "For it is not as so oft considered," said Cayce, "that the family of the Master lacked material opportunities. For from many sources there had come the opportunities for those in the household of the Master to have the greater training."

With the varying influences in her life, Ruth, in those early periods, "was divided in thought and activity between those tenets held by the elder brother, James, those held by the mother, and the actual activities of herself as one among a peoples that were being questioned and doubted."

There seems to have been doubt in her mind as to ideas—but apparently none as to the ideal, "I am my brother's keeper," for, Cayce said, "As the circumstances from the material angles began to alter, or the position of the family began to change . . .", Ruth experienced "the necessity of expending self's efforts mentally, materially, for the aid and understanding of those that are in less fortunate circumstances from the worldly angle, or to bring a knowledge to those in sundry places as to the cooperation that might be attained or gained by those in such circumstances with those in authority politically as well as religiously." Or, in short, she "ministered to those that were in want, that were in need of the material things."

With the return of John, the cousin, and the beginning of his ministry, the preaching in the wilderness, rather than serving in the temple, "there was brought consternation" to Ruth. "And again there was a questioning with the mother as to those experiences of the mother preceding the birth of Jesus."

Then came "the return of Jesus to the Palestine Land, after those periods of the tests in the wilderness, after his meeting with John; and then the return to Capernaum and the teaching that he, Jesus, accorded there."

Returning from that meeting where Ruth first heard her brother speak publicly, and witnessed the disturbance thus created, Ruth encountered a young Roman official, "a collector, not in the sense of the 'taker in,' but the supervisor as to the abilities of various individuals in various positions to pay that tribute," a man named Philoas. The introduction was made at that meeting by one who was "a minister to the bodily needs of those whom oft Ruth, as well as the then new companion, had met."

Accompanied by those two companions, Ruth "returned immediately to the home and acquainted Mary with what had taken place, warning her of the possible entanglements with the Roman authorities, or the Roman activities."

It might be wondered why the Roman authorities might take issue in this matter. It should be remembered that, while the Romans were little concerned with the religious beliefs or practices of the peoples of their subjugated provinces, they were concerned with keeping the peace or maintaining order, which had proven to be no small matter in this riot-prone province. And, since the religious outlook of these people was the basis of much of their unrest, as indeed of all their activity, any religious situation producing serious anger might be the spark to set off a conflagration which it was the duty of the Roman occupational forces to prevent.

Philoas' concern in the matter, however, according to Cayce's account, was not only due to his official duties, for he soon came to have a personal interest in the young woman, Ruth. "Being not only beautiful in body, but active in seeking to alleviate those conditions that were accorded to those people in the less fortunate circumstance, which became a part of the interests of that unusual Roman, the natural consequence of the age, the material circumstance, brought about a bond of sympathy between the two."

Philoas must, indeed, have been an "unusual Roman," as well as one most important in the experience of the followers of the Christ. He had been born in that portion of the land under Roman rule that was a portion of Heliopolis, as the "son of one Antonius and Josie, in the activities of the Roman experience, and was educated in the ways of those peoples that were both from the Roman and the Grecian forces. And those things that became a part of the experiences, the character, were the lessons that had been taught by that Grecian soldier that later was fed the hemlock." By this, of course, Cayce referred to the teachings of Socrates, whose ideas and idealistic philosophy provided the basis for much of the ethical thoughts and reasoning since his time.

Philoas "grew into grace with those in authority," Cayce says, "through the activities as came under the influence of Caesar Augustus, and later Claudius, and those that ruled over the varied lands that had become a portion of that under the direction of the Romans." He became "one who traveled through those lands," as a representative of the Roman people, "not as a tax gatherer, but to judge the conditions, the situations of the various groups and as to their abilities to contribute, not only the fruits of their labors but of their activities in the various fields of service." While he was not in direct authority over the people, "not as a soldier, not as a lord or king," it was his duty or function to make "those recommendations for the manners in which the peoples under the various schools would be taxed, according to their spiritual counsel . . . or according to what ye would call the religious influences and the judging of these."

Here is another reference pointing to the impossibility of separating the religious and civil affairs in this land. For, from the standpoint of the people themselves, the rulership of the religious leaders was that which was accepted without rebellion; therefore, it was expedient for the Romans to do much of their governing of the country through the cooperation of the "religious influences."

"During those periods," Cayce says, "the activities were in keeping the Jewish masters or the Jewish rulers coordinating with the activities of the Roman rulers. . . ." This necessitated acquiring a thorough understanding of the religious associations or affiliations of the people, the attitudes of the different groups toward the Roman and Jewish rule. So Philoas "studied, as it were, those things that prompted the activity of the various sets and sects, as the Pharisees, the Sadducees, the Essenes; the influence upon the Roman soldiery as well as the Roman rule, as well as upon individuals who were set in authority in the varied provinces."

So when Philoas, at the age of thirty, first came into association with Ruth, "during those periods when the Master walked in the earth . . . as the young man just beginning the ministry," much of that which had been "a portion of the experience of the household of Mary and Joseph was known to him. For, owing to the visitation of Jesus, the man, in other lands, and because of the Roman rule and the changes wrought, Philoas then found it necessary to make for the activities, the inquiries that brought a closer understanding."

Some of these inquiries had been made of Judy, at that time the head of the Essenes, and from her Philoas "gained or obtained a record of that as had been gathered by the keeper of records from Carmel." These inquiries included those "respecting the activities of the Essenes, as to whether they were averse to the authority of the Jewish rulers, as well as the Romans." And "not as an informer was Philoas considered by Judy, but as one that would and did give the facts of the activities of the various groups in respect to not only the Essenes, but the other portions of the various groups in the land."

When Ruth's associations with Philoas had advanced "from those periods of the first timidity of Ruth," she experienced "some resentment towards the mother as to the advice or council given," that the association with this man, "one of other or foreign or alien groups," not be continued.

Mary's advice to Ruth is very understandable. The Romans were not only, to most Jews, the hated occupiers of their country, but impious and abominable heathen, who were, according to the Jewish law, considered unclean. While the Essenes did not hold to all the precepts of the orthodox groups, in most cases they were just as strict in their observance of the laws of purity or cleanliness. Ruth, however, as indicated earlier, did not hold strictly to the beliefs of either of the Jewish groups, and her attitude concerning the association with aliens had undoubtedly been influenced greatly by her education in Greece and Rome. Her mother's counsel notwithstanding, she followed her own ideas in the matter.

"There was the persistence in the activities," Cayce says, "for to Ruth the new-found friend bespoke a greater knowledge of the needs of human experience than that held to by either the Essenes or the orthodox Jewish peoples. Hence the continuations of those activities in association oft with that friend."

As a natural result of Philoas's activity, "as one associated with the producer and that produced, or with capital and labor, or the activities related to same," many of the tax gatherers, the tax assessors, and "those who judged in the various provinces as to the amounts, as to the abilities," came under his supervision. Matthew, who became one of the disciples, the apostles, of Jesus, was one of these, for he "had been appointed as an aide" of Philoas. Many of the other disciples became acquaintances of Philoas, in one manner or another, and many became close friends.

"It is sometimes judged that most of the disciples were poor," Cayce says, "and this was not true. Zebedee and his sons, Matthew, the publican, all who were closely associated were rather well-to-do." Peter and Andrew were servants or laborers with the sons of Zebedee, and were not actually wealthy, nor were Thomas and Alpheus, but these were closely associated with those who "were in authority so far as capital is concerned." Hence the association of Philoas with the disciples, and "in these conditions did Philoas come under the influence of the Prince of Peace, the teachings of the Nazarene," becoming ever more closely associated with those of the household of Jesus. And in his "services to the people, to the nation," he was "not as one that acted in those capacities as one in a passive manner, but ever as the positive, as the active influence in the experiences that came under the visions, the experiences of the man, Jesus, as a teacher, as a healer."

When the days of the Passover feast had come, and Jesus went into Jerusalem, as indicated in the Gospels, there was much interest aroused by the miracles of healing he performed there.

Undoubtedly, there were many there who had previously heard of this man, this rabbi, the master or initiate of the mysteries of Egypt. One such, according to Cayce, was the Pharisee Nicodemus. For Martha, the wife of Nicodemus, was an Essene, and had known of the prophecies concerning Jesus, and their fulfillment.

In those days when the Essenes had been looking forward to the advent of the promised Messiah into the earth, and Judy had been the leader of those groups banded together to study the prophecies and reckonings of that which was to take place, Martha's mother and sister had had the experience of coming in touch with Judy, and their interest was reflected in the daily conversation in their home.

Since Martha, at that time, was still a child, or "in those periods of development," Cayce said, "these had become a part of what would today be called a play-experience for Martha." Although her sister, Esdrella, was many years her senior, and no longer a child to take part in such play, "the coming of John, the birth of Jesus, the dispensation of Jesus and John in Egypt, all had an impression or imprint upon the mind of Martha, who builded in her own mind how the announcer of the king should be dressed, as this had been a part of the experiences of Martha in other periods, and thus the choice of things in this direction.

"Then there came those great changes in the life experience of Martha. For one among those of the rulers of the synagogue sought her hand in marriage, and through the individuals who made these arrangements, Martha was espoused to Nicodemus." Thus Nicodemus first learned of what had happened in the homes of John the Baptist, and of Mary and Joseph and Jesus.

And then Esdrella's son-in-law, Simon the fisherman of Galilee, had become a disciple of the Master, this worker of miracles who had come now to Jerusalem.

So, as recorded in the Gospel of John, Nicodemus went by night to question him. For, though his interest is understandable, his position as a member of the Sanhedrin, the council of the Jews, and as a ruler of the synagogue, made advisable that his interest in this unorthodox teacher be not made publicly known.

Then came the well-known teaching of Jesus, "ye must be born again—Ye must be born of water and of the

Spirit," and the conversation or explanation by Jesus which followed when Nicodemus failed to understand.

Even with Jesus' explanation, the lesson apparently is still poorly understood. For this, though one of the most often quoted passages of the Bible, is also one of the most disputed.

As Cayce pointed out, "A background of the whole setting makes this better understood. Nicodemus was among those of the Sanhedrin, those of the teachers, those of the elders, with that privilege of having access to all that had been given from the ordinances that were delivered to Moses on the mount—the relationships of individuals and the relationships of the individual soul to its maker, though much had come to be as omens or heresy, rather than the ordinances of old.

"When Nicodemus asked, 'How can such things be?' the rebuke came in his answer, 'Art thou a teacher in Israel and knoweth not these things?'

"We must be born of water, of blood. Or of the spirit and through the flesh. Or that all must pass under the rod; even as was given by those teachers, that as Moses and the children passed through the sea they were baptized in the cloud, in the sea, as an example, as an omen, as a physical activity of a spiritual, a physical separation from that which had been builded in their experience as the sojourn in Egypt.

"As the Master gave to Nicodemus, ye must be born of the spirit where ye may make manifest the fruits of the spirit. Where? In the earth! Not that these come in their order as indicated in the question by Nicodemus, but in their relative position as to their development, their necessities, their needs for their soul growth, their soul understanding.

"Oh that all would gather more of that understanding that the soul is a body and the physical is the mere temple, the mere shell, the mere material manifestation of that which may not be touched by hands! For it ap-

90

pears that we must be born again that we may dwell in those mansions not made with hands, but are prepared for those that have washed their robes, their bodies, their souls in the blood.

"For ye are ones that may know the truth, if ye will but manifest in thine own experiences that ye have learned in thine meditations with thy God.

"Ye must be born in flesh, in spirit again, that ye may make manifest that ye have experienced in thine own soul!"

After that Passover season during which Nicodemus had visited him, Jesus remained with his disciples in Judea for a time, according to the Gospels, and large numbers of people flocked to him. The experiences of Sarapha that Cayce describes give further insight as to attitudes and events of that period.

"Throughout the preparation of the Master," Sarapha had "wondered and sought word as to his progress in following that which had become almost as a story; yet she held to those visions, those experiences in the evening before, and during those periods when they beheld the light, when they beheld the Child in the mother's arms—and then that glorious moment when it had been placed in her own, and she had pressed her lips to the brow of that babe.

"When there had begun, then, the ministry of Jesus the man, Sarapha had held fast to these, and stayed close to every word that might be gathered from those who heard the more oft," though "the rejection by his own people brought tears of scalding shame to Sarapha for those very ones that seemed to doubt when they should know." For, said Cayce, there were doubts, fears, and not-understandings as to why other members of the family, especially, could not see in the child, the man, that which had been experienced by Sarapha.

"But when the visits brought him near to the home on the edge of Olivet, and yet the cares kept her closer to

the abode, the inn near the highways through which
throngs now oft passed, where Sarapha ministered to
the needs of the travelers, she pondered, grew fearful for
the things that were being said." For the miracles that were
wrought, and the great following that he began to have,
and the knowledge of his association with John and that
persecuted group or sect of which John was the head,
had aroused the interest, the concern, the anger of the
Pharisees.

For, as is recorded in the Gospel of John, some of
the Pharisees, going into that area where John was baptizing, at Aenon in Samaria, began disputing with his
disciples concerning purification, and when they reported
to John on the size or extent of the following of Jesus,
John again bore witness to the Master, saying, "He must
increase, and I must decrease."

Then Herod threw John into prison, because of his
public condemnation of Herod's taking his brother's wife,
or, in Cayce's words, "that there might be the appeasing
of a selfish desire, because he, John, had spoken against
that which answered to the aggrandizing of a fleshly lust."
Again, then, according to Cayce, the Essenes, John's
followers, were persecuted and questioned because of those
charges made by John against those in political authority; and Roael, the elder son of Zebedee, "was among
those that suffered persecution and death." But Herod,
held between fear and anger of John's condemnation, and
the fear and awe of John as a prophet, a man of God,
delayed and hesitated in making a decision concerning
him, and for a time refused the counsel of those close to
him that John should be put to death. He allowed John
visitors in prison, and Sofa, who had been his nurse in
his childhood, and had been among the first to be bap-
tised by him, ministered to his needs in prison.

The Bible tells how, when Jesus had heard of these
things, he left Judea and went again into Galilee. And

young through gr... nev-
er grow old. These books include
Utopia by Thomas More; the complete works of Shakespeare; Benjamin Franklin's Autobiography;
Omar Khayyam's Rubaiyat; Wal-
den by Thoreau; and other fresh,
spontaneous, even outspoken works
that stretch your mind and sweep
away the mental cobwebs that hold
back most men.

You never have to buy any of
these books. (To force you to buy a
classic would be barbaric.) As a
member, take only those books you
really want to own. And, at any time,
you may cancel your membership,
without penalty or hurt feelings.

(Continued on other side) →

First Class
Permit No. 7
Roslyn, N.Y.

BUSINESS REPLY MAIL
No postage stamp necessary if mailed in the United States

Postage Will Be Paid By

THE CLASSICS CLUB
Roslyn, New York 11576

for the introductory price of $1.00, plus shipping.

We know what charmers these three wise men are. We are betting that you will be so taken by them that you will want to stay in the Club and meet some of their friends, including the greatest story tellers, philosophers, poets and historians the world has ever known.

Do not send any money now. We'll bill you later. Just fill in and mail the attached postage-paid card, today, while you are thinking about it and while the invitation still stands.

THE CLASSICS CLUB
Roslyn, New York 11576

Please enroll me as a Trial Member, and send me at once the THREE beautiful Classics Club Editions of PLATO, ARISTOTLE AND MARCUS AURELIUS. I enclose NO MONEY; within a week after receiving my books, I will either return them and owe nothing, or keep them for the special introductory price of ONLY $1.00 (plus a few cents mailing charges) for ALL THREE.

As a member, I am to receive advance descriptions of all future selections, but am not obligated to buy any. For each volume I keep, I will send you only $3.89 (plus a few cents mailing charges). I may reject any volume before or after I receive it, and cancel my membership at any time.

Mr., Mrs., Miss _____
(Please Print Plainly)

Address _____

City _____ State _____ Zip _____

In Canada: Enclose this reply card in an envelope and mail to CLASSICS CLUB OF CANADA, Pendragon House Ltd., 71 Bathurst Street, Toronto 135, Ontario passing through Samaria, he came to the city called Sychar, and talked there to a woman at the well.

This woman, according to Cayce, was named Jodie, and she and her sisters, Selma and Josie, were of the household of Pagosius, "a ruler, or one in command of those that administered the secular laws of the land," and "of the kingdoms of those of Syria, to whom Samaria had paid tribute," though now "under the rule of the Romans, to whom all Palestine paid tribute in that day."

These people of Samaria, Cayce points out, were "the mixture of the Edomites and the Jewish people left when the first of these were carried into captivity. With the return of those first under Zerubbabel, and the dispersing as happened by Sanballat and Loti, as teachers in Seir, these were called then the Samaritans, and Seir—where Jeroboam had builded an altar—was chosen as the place for the people to worship."

So, as in the common version of the incident of the woman at the well, Cayce says, there was the question to the Master, "Ye say in Jerusalem is the place to worship; our fathers, Mt. Seir." And the answer came, "Not in this mountain, nor yet in Jerusalem—but even in thine own heart may be the awakening, quickened by the love of the Father through the Son for an erring and unstable child." And with the awakening did Jodie "bring into the minds, hearts and souls, first of her own household, then of the multitudes, then of the greater masses, that of the beauty of life in Him, of the glories of the Father in Him."

"That accomplished" in Jodie and Josie and Selma, as the result of this contact with the Master, was "of the twofold nature; overcoming of not only that of the hatred of those of another race, but also the overcoming of self in its exultant, exalted opinion, on account of birth and position."

"The teachings of the man of Nazareth to these peoples," Cayce said, "began with this household," and with the spreading of the glad tidings to the people of Mt. Seir by Selma, the sister of Jodie, and those that heeded the lessons that were gained through that meeting at the well, there was the establishing in Samaria "of groups nearer akin to those of the synagogue, or that which would be termed the daily or cottage prayer meetings."

"As for the tidings given . . . in that period, there may be found a record in Josephus, as well as the stories among the writings of one Bartimaeus in the Jewish history, in which there is given the variation of how or what effect is had upon those particular people. The intent, as is seen, is the influence, the different effects had upon individual minds by the teachings of this man, this teacher, this leader."

The teachings, as given to others by those who heard his message at Sychar, Cayce says, "were the following of that belief as set by Him, that He *was* the light that came into the world to show the way of approach to the kingdom—as lies within. How that animosity, hatred of those that were considered not of a pure race might be cleansed every whit in the giving of self wholly to the ministering of the Lamb—that took away the sins of the world, that made the paths straight, that brought healing to the weary in body and mind, brought love where hatred existed, brought love where there was former considerations of time, place, relations; brought love to those despised of men for weaknesses of the flesh, who were made strong in the love of Him, the Christ."

According to the Bible, when Jesus returned to Galilee he came again to the seashore and called to Peter and Andrew, and James and John, that they should leave their nets and follow him. And he came to the place where the customs were collected, and spoke to Matthew, a keeper of the custom, or tax collector, that he should follow him. And these, from this time on, stayed close in the association with the Master.

With these and others of his disciples he came to Cana, and Capernaum, and throughout Galilee, teaching the Word of the Father, healing all kinds of diseases, and cleansing many of the demons or devils or unclean spirits with which they were possessed.

The Gospels abound with the stories of such healings. They were considered miracles—yet there was also his promise, "He that believeth on me, the works that I do shall he do also."

From the Cayce readings comes information which may provide greater understanding of the underlying principles of healing, the spiritual laws that both make possible these "miracles" that Jesus performed, and make possible the fulfilment of that promise.

All life, Cayce said, is the manifestation of Creative forces or the expression of Divine influences in a material world. And that same power that creates is the power, the only power, that can bring healing. All healing forces are within, and all healing is the attuning of each atom of the body, each reflex of the brain, to the awareness of the Divine that lies within each atom, each cell. The power is in Him, the Creator. The power needed by all is the realization of abiding in His presence.

Then, through the complete realization of the presence of the Father, the Creative Force abiding within, the awareness that "I and the Father are one," came the power of Jesus to perform the miracles of healing, to so affect the consciousness of the individual as to allow that healing to take place. Yet material applications were sometimes necessary, as in the case of the blind man, whose eyes Jesus annointed with clay mixed with spittle. For the consciousness of the individual had to be taken into consideration, and "applications from without," as Cayce said, "are merely to create within a coordinating mental and spiritual force."

These principles explain, somewhat, the relation of sin

to illness, inasmuch as sin affects the consciousness of the individual as to his relationship to the Creator.

Cayce refers, in other cases, more directly to the relationship of the forgiveness of sin to the healing of illness. "There were many instances," he said, "where individual healings by the Master were of the nature as to be instantaneous, as that when he said to him sick of the palsy, 'Son, thy sins be forgiven thee.' When the questions came, as he knew they would, he answered, 'Which is it easier to say, 'Thy sins be forgiven thee,' or 'Take up thy bed and go unto thine house?' Immediately the man arose, took up his bed and went into his house! Here we find it was not by the command, but by his own personage. For the question was not as to whether he healed, but as to whether he had the power to forgive sin. The recognition was that sin had caused the physical disturbance.

"Then these are part of the experience of each and every soul in their search for, in their relationships with, their fellow man."

"The Master in many cases forgave sins in healing individuals," Cayce said. "For sins are of commission and omission. Sins of commission were forgiven, while sins of omission were called to mind, even by the Master."

As the Master's fame and popularity increased, according to the account in the Gospels, so too—among some factions—did opposition and hatred. The Pharisees and the Herodians began to plot together how they might find cause to put him to death. For the Herodians, that political party which favored the rule of Herod and the dependence upon Rome, feared Jesus's influence with the people. And because he healed on the Sabbath, thus (in the eyes of the Pharisees, those so righteous in their own opinion) breaking the Sabbath, they condemned him— and especially were they outraged when he called himself the Son of God.

How are we to interpret this statement of the Master,

that he was, that he is the Son of God? In several of the readings of Cayce explanations of this are given:

"As we have given, and as was given by him, in the beginning he was the Son—made the Son—those of the Sons that went astray; and through the varying activities overcame the world through the experiencies."

By this it would seem that he, Jesus, was not the only son. Indeed, both the Bible and the Cayce material indicate that we, each one, may be considered as the sons of the Creator. Yet Jesus was referred to in the Bible as the "only begotten Son." This apparent discrepancy may be better understood by considering the following statements made by Cayce:

"When there was the beginning of man's advent into the plane known as the earth, and he became a living soul, amenable to the laws that governed the plane itself, as presented, the Son of Man entered the earth as the first man, the son of man, the Son of God, the Son of the First Cause making manifest in a material body. This was not the first spiritual influence, spiritual body, spiritual manifestation in the earth, but the first man— flesh and blood; the first carnal house, the first body amenable to the laws of the plane in its position in the universe.

"For the earth is only an atom in the universe of worlds. And man's development began through the laws of the generations in the earth . . . Hence, as there came the development of that first entity of flesh and blood through the earth plane, he became indeed the Son—through the things which he experienced in the varied planes, as the development came to the oneness with the position in that which man terms the Triune.

"In that the man, Jesus, became the ensample of the flesh, manifest in the world, and the will one with the Father, he became the first to manifest same in the material world. Thus, from man's viewpoint, becoming the only, the first begotten of the Father, religious forces."

97

According to the Gospel of John, at the time that Jesus so angered the Pharisees by calling himself the Son of God he also made a wonderful promise: "The dead shall hear the voice of the Son of God, and they shall live." And soon came the first fulfillment of that promise —the raising up of the daughter of Jairus.

This girl, according to Cayce, was named Toupar, and the story of the family is given in some detail. Her mother, Maipah, "was among the daughters of the children of Ishmael. And the associations, the wedding with Jairus in the early portions of Maipah's experience in the earth plane came about through the journeying of Jairus with those influences established in the western portion of the country now known as Turkey.

"There was quite a variation as to the position of women in a household such as that of Maipah and those in the household of those in authority, as was Jairus, because of his position politically. He was not merely the captain of a guard or of a garrison, but as one who was in authority pertaining to the supplying of the commercial, the social and the political relationships of the land, when Maipah joined in the activities in portions of that now known as the Galilean land."

Maipah "was some twenty years of age when the first child was born; then the second and third, which was the daughter, Toupar.

"When the husband, Jairus, became aware of the teachings of the Master, Jesus of Nazareth, and knowing of the conditions surrounding the companion, and the 'delicate condition,' as would be called (for there was the expectancy of the fourth child to be born) the anxiety as manifested brought commendation from the Master, as well as the wonderment from his associates or companions in his office. For this showed rather an unusual interest of man for his mate and for the offspring for that period of time. But Jairus had been influenced by those

98

tenets which he had heard expressed, not only by John, but by the followers of, and the Master himself.

"This brought into the experience of Maipah that of humbleness, patience, desire for expression in some manner. Yet, because of the early teaching, the early training, wonderment and fear and doubt were also a part of the consciousness through that particular period."

And then, when there was the illness and death of the daughter, though the Master came to the home and said that she, the child, was not dead, "with the conditions and environs of self as well as the counsel or advice of others, there came doubt and fear. Yet with the command that those that would hinder by their adverse thought or expressions be put away, Maipah and Jairus had their loved one given to them as a living example of his (the Christ) being indeed the resurrection and the life."

Another instance given in the Gospels of the raising of the dead by Jesus was that of the raising of the son of the widow of Nain, who was, according to Cayce, a relative of Nicodemus.

The news of these miracles, as might be expected, brought awe and fear, and spread far and wide. John, in prison, learned of the miracles from his disciples. Then, as recorded by Matthew and Luke, John sent to Jesus two of his disciples who asked, "Are you he for whom we have waited?"

These two disciples, according to Cayce, were Sopha and John's sister, Adahr. There had been, Cayce said, much "doubt and confusion in the experience of Adahr, owing to the teachings of the priests and the rejecting of same by the brother and his acceptance of the teachings of the Essenes; and only in those answers that came to the inner self was there brought an understanding. For through Adahr's own expression and seeking there came that answer, 'Go tell John the things ye have seen and heard—the lame walk, the blind see, the sick are healed, the poor have the gospel preached to them.' Then there came in Adahr's experience the full meaning of the priesthood in Israel, and how that the lowly Nazarene was that fulfilling of that priesthood in his offering of himself as the lamb that was not to roll back but to take away the sins of the people. Not as an escape, but as an atonement in which each soul does find, would find, the lamb standing ever as that offering in its relationship as an individual to its fellow man."

But with the answers given, Sofa "was confused until those reclaiming activities upon the day of Pentecost," and she returned to John in prison, and was among the chief mourners when he was beheaded.

Some of those Romans in authority in Palestine, said Cayce, were in that land because of their position as "a helpful influence for the people of that land, as well as for the influences or forces or powers of other lands." The wife of one of these Romans was a woman named Elcor, of Grecian descent, and it was in her home and through the associations with her household that Jesus first came into contact with one of the interesting and important New Testament characters.

The experience of Elcor herself, as given in a reading by Cayce, is interesting as to the attitudes and reactions toward Jesus and his followers.

"When there was the voicing of groups and individuals as to that fact taking place, of a new teacher, at first this was considered [by Elcor] merely as something of the same thing which had been as a report of those peoples for many, many years. Yet with the contact in a social manner, and in the manners in which needs were applied in healings . . . Elcor began to consider those teachings and influences from a different angle.

"Because of the character or manner of livelihood of many of those who were proclaimed as disciples of this new teacher, the Nazarene, Elcor attempted to dismiss them. However, again and again she was presented with those influences proclaimed by groups as to the experiences and the life of that individual, and as to the followers being in that position of fulfilling the prophecies which had been a part of not only the teachings of those peculiar peoples, but also of the verse and the songs of the peoples of many lands.

"Though many of those groups were oft questionable to Elcor, these had an altering influence in her experience; sometimes doubting, sometimes fearing, sometimes dismissing."

For, Jesus's activities progressed, "there were periods of fear that there might be an uprising, such as to undermine the very foundations of that upon which she and her associates and her household depended."

"Note the meaning," Cayce comments, "of the name Elcor: one who joined doubt with faith." So, in spite of doubts and fears, she did not reject Jesus or his teachings. She was often "in the presence of the Master when he spoke in places where those in authority entertained, and he was in Elcor's own home when the woman of the street was questioned by one of the companions there. This experience brought confusion and yet determinations in her experience."

This woman, Cayce says, who was brought before the Roman authorities there, was Mary Magdalene, Mary, the sister of Martha and Lazarus of Bethany. But she had become "a courtesan that was active in the experience both of those that were in the capacity of the Roman officers, Roman peoples, and those that were of the native lands and country."

Mary had "set about what would be called now a home for or retreat for those who sought to use and give their bodies to those activities for the indulgences and for the gaining of information of various sorts or natures through such activities of the individuals."

In just what way this information was used or turned to profit was not given by Cayce, but it was apparently very profitable from the material standpoint, for these activities of Mary and her associates, though being those that "brought condemnation," brought as well "the pomp, the power, the splendor, when considered from that angle."

These activities also made Mary a potentially dangerous influence in the affairs of many whose activities were such that there were reasons they should not be made known. Perhaps that was the reason for the accusations being made against her.

The reason for her being questioned by those in Roman authority in the household of Elcor on this occasion when she first met the Master was that the council, or court at the time, had brought her, asking that, according to the Jewish law, the woman be stoned. And Jesus, being known as a Jewish Rabbi, was questioned as to the law of Moses concerning such activities.

And Jesus stooped and wrote upon the ground "that which condemned each individual as each looked over his arm as he wrote." For that which was written "made the accusers recognize their own activities."

Mary was described by Cayce as being "five feet four inches in height, weight a hundred and twenty pounds, hair almost red; the eyes were blue. The features were those impelled both from the Grecian and Jewish ancestry."

She was twenty-three years old, said Cayce, "when the Christ cleansed her from the seven devils—hate, avarice, self-indulgence and those of the kindred selfishness, hopelessness and blasphemy.

"With the cleansing of the body mind, through the association and experience, Mary joined again with those of the family from which she had been separated in Bethany and became then again of the household of those that dwelt there."

No scene or conversation, Cayce said, had greater value to this entity than the words of the Master, "Neither do I condemn thee." For this awakened within her soul the love and the oneness of the force or power able to cleanse, when condemnation is not in self.

"Hence, as given then, and as had been given oft—do not condemn self. For as each soul learns, condemning self is condemning the abilities of the Master."

Frequent references were made in the Cayce readings to the "Holy Women," many individuals being told that they had been "among the Holy Women" during this period when the Master walked in the earth. No reference is found in the Bible concerning such a group, and Cayce does not make it clear as to whether this was an organized group or merely a term used to indicate those who dedicated their lives, their activities to the service of God and His Messiah.

Maipah, the wife of Jairus, Cayce said, "sought to know and aid those who were the leaders or teachers, of course the Holy Women, the prophetesses, and those who had been instrumental in every form or manner in keeping the tenets alive in the experience of others."

This function of the Holy Women as teachers is illustrated in the experience of Eloise. "When there were those who gathered to listen, to seek not only physical but mental and spiritual relief and understanding," Cayce said, she, among those of the Holy Women, "kept the school on the way above Emmaus, to the way that 'goeth down towards Jericho' and towards the northernmost coast from Jerusalem." She was then "in close acquaint-anceship with many who were the teachers, or the apostles, or the disciples, and many of those women, as Mary, Martha, Elizabeth; all of these were as friends, yea, companions." She was then "what would be termed in the present, in some organizations, as a Sister Superior, or an officer, as it were, in those of the Essenes and their preparations.

"Hence we find Eloise then, giving, giving, ministering, encouraging, making for the greater activities, and making for those encouraging experiences oft in the lives of the disciples, coming in contact with the Master oft in the ways between Bethany, Galilee, Jerusalem." She "blessed many of those who came to seek to know the teachings, the ways, the mysteries, the understandings," for she "had been trained in the schools of those that were of the prophets and prophetesses, and was indeed a prophetess in those experiences."

Some of the Holy Women ministered to the Master personally, following him from place to place. Josie, who had been the handmaid to Mary and cared for Jesus in his early years, "was known among the Holy Women throughout the period," and apparently kept close to him much of the time.

Of particular aid to and among the Holy Women was Martha, the wife of Nicodemus. In the activities of Martha, when Nicodemus had gone to the Master by night, there began "those discussions in the home." And there had begun, then, for Martha and Nicodemus, "the communion as of man and wife, rather than of man and his chattel or servant. They were more on a basis of equality, not in the same proportions which were established a bit later by some of the rulers from the Roman land, but more in keeping with the happenings which had brought about the activities in the Essenes group."

Though Nicodemus "never accepted completely the tenets or teachings of the Essene group," Martha held to and applied those principles. She was a friend of Mary, Elizabeth, and the other Mary, and because of her position as the wife of Nicodemus she was "considered as one of the leaders, or one to whom others made appeal to have positions or conditions set in motion so that there was given more concessions to the Holy Women who followed Jesus from place to place when there were those periods of his Palestine ministry."

One of those women who followed Jesus from place to place was Susane, "not one that would in this day or period be termed a nun, but one ministering first-hand as a nurse, as one working with the hands."

Since Susane and her family were closely associated with both the family of the Master and several of the important events of the period of his ministry as recorded in the Bible, much of the information from the Cayce readings concerning them is given here.

Susane was a daughter of Cleopas, one of those who "had been appointed from Rome as collectors of the various forms of tax as imposed upon and collected from the peoples." Since he was "among those that were of the faith of the peoples of that land, as had been Matthew . . . he was in that environ or that shadow, as may be termed, of one professing a faith in the teachings of the Scribes and Pharisees, yet collecting the tribute for a power over the peoples. This brought condemnation to many of the household, then, from those who adhered more to the orthodox manner of living or activity."

Susane, however, growing up during that period of the early life of the Master in the earth, became acquainted with those of the household of Mary and Joseph, for the family of Susane "was of the city of Capernaum at that time."

Susane was near the age of Ruth, the sister of the Master, "and there were the close acquaintanceships and friendships, though there were the various degrees of associations, owing to those questions as arose in the various groups that were of the synagogue activities. There were the close companionships, though, until there were the separations owing to the varied manners of education of the two."

Susane, therefore, "knew a great deal about the happenings in that household. The acquaintanceships with Jude and James was also a part of her experience" during those early years.

Susane, "more than most of the Holy Women—as they were eventually called, years afterward—followed the teachings of the Master under the various circumstances, being in the areas about Bethsaida in that period of the expression manifested when there was the feeding of the five thousand and when there was the rebuking of the peoples that were especially about Judas at that time."

Susane was one of these, for "in the beginning Susane rather favored the manner in which those groups about Judas sought to proclaim Jesus as the deliverer of the people from that bondage, that taxation" of Rome, though this, as was natural considering the occupation of her father, brought to her "condemnation from her own groups of peoples."

Then came that experience, recorded in the Gospels and recounted by Cayce, "when there were those gatherings about the mount in the wilderness and the call of the five thousand that they be sent not away in their weakness, but the supplying of the physical needs to the material man."

When Jesus instructed his disciples to see how much food was available, Ardoen, the son of Andrew, says Cayce, brought to his father a lad, his companion, who had the loaves and fishes, "that there might be supplied from that which he had in hand sufficient of the material needs to feed that multitude."

When these were distributed, as related by the Gospels, and seen to be sufficient, even more than sufficient for the needs of all, many of those people henceforth followed Jesus for the sake of the loaves and fishes, or the hope of the material benefits this miracle worker might provide.

Then, as they followed after him and attempted to proclaim him king, Jesus rebuked them, "Ye seek me because ye ate and were filled." And Susane, said Cayce, "was reminded of her association in the household of the Master, and the purposes for which this entrance in the world had been—as he gave, not for self, not for material gain, but that all should know the truth that would make all men free under every circumstance in a material plane."

According to the account in the Bible, as the rumors spread among the people concerning Jesus's miracles, Herod, the Tetrarch of Galilee, was much perplexed. For it was rumored that John the Baptist, whom Herod had beheaded, had risen again from the dead, or that Elias or some other of the prophets of old, risen again, was he who did these wonders. Herod, perhaps because of his guilt and fear, apparently held more to the belief that it was indeed John.

Yet when Jesus, knowing of these rumors and the confusion that had arisen in the minds of many, asked his disciples, "Whom say ye that I am?" then came that answer from Peter, that answer so meaningful, so wonderful, so full of hope, of joy, of triumph to all the world: "Thou art the Christ!"

Yea, he was, he *is* the Christ, says Cayce, yet also the man, the Son of Man, born of Mary, tempted in all ways as we are.

Since we are told that Jesus is the Christ, and indeed he is often referred to in the Bible as Jesus Christ, the words are often used synonymously. Yet this, according to the philosophy of the Cayce readings, is not correct. Cayce differentiates between the two words and explains the meaning of each.

"Jesus is the man," he said, "the activity, the mind, the relationships that he bore to others. Yes, he was mindful of friends, he was sociable, he was loving, he was kind, he was gentle. He grew faint, he grew weak, and yet gained that strength that he has promised in becoming the Christ by fulfilling and overcoming the world. We are made strong in body, in mind, in soul and purpose by that power in Christ. The power, then, is in the Christ. The pattern is in Jesus!"

"Christ is not a man!" Cayce said in another reading. "Jesus was the man; Christ the messenger. Christ in all ages—Jesus in one, Joshua in another, Melchizedek in another; these be those that led Judaism! These be they that came as that Child of Promise, as to the Children of Promise."

The Christ Spirit, not the man, said Cayce, should be the Door, the Truth, the Way. When asked to explain this and expand it, he answered:

"That which has been given may be used to illustrate the difference that may be felt by a soul that has become aware of itself, as the Christ, or as Jesus the man became aware of the Spirit of the Father through those experiences of the man as he 'went about doing good,' and at those periods when there was received those acknowledgments of the Father that he was the one who could, would, through those activities, become the savior of man. First, as 'in whom I am well pleased,' then as 'This is my son; hear ye him.' "

Cayce also differentiated between the Christ Spirit and the Christ Consciousness. "As the difference might be given," he said, "in that which makes for the birth in the flower, and the flower. The consciousness of the Spirit and the abilities to apply same are the differences in the Christ Consciousness, the Christ Spirit.

"As has been given, the devils believe, the devils know, individuals may be conscious of an activity. Those with the abilities to call upon, to be so unselfish as to allow the Spirit to operate in self's stead, are aware of the Spirit's activity, while those that may be conscious or aware of a truth may not wholly make it their own without that which has been given, 'He that would have life must give life;' for he thought it not robbery to be equal with the Father, yet of himself did nothing, but 'the Father that worketh in me, through me.' Do thou likewise, that thou may know the consciousness of the Christ Spirit, and experience the operation of that witness that 'my spirit beareth witness with thy spirit, that the Father may be glorified in you, even as I am glorified in the

Father through you. I will not leave thee comfortless; I will make thee aware of that glory I possessed with the Father before the world was.'

"In such a manner may individuals become aware of the Christ Consciousness and become one with the operative forces of the Christ Spirit abroad in the earth; for he shall come again, even as ye have seen him go. Then shall the Christ Spirit be manifest in the world, even as the Christ Consciousness may make thee aware of that promised as the Comforter in this material world.

"Then, the Christ Consciousness is the Holy Spirit, or that as the promise of his presence making aware of his activity in the earth. The spirit is as the Christ in action with the Spirit of the Father."

Cayce's explanation of the meaning of "the Christ" seems closely related to the statement in the first part of the Gospel of John, that the Christ was "the true light that lighteth every man that cometh into the world."

"Consider all of those things given of old," Cayce said, "in comparison to that taught by the Master, which is that to be gained by each and every entity in the present; that it is not from without where there may be visions, voices or what not, but it is the light that comes from within.

"This he taught, this he manifested; that it is not a dependence upon the powers without! Remember the great lesson taught in that record given or indicated to those who were with him at that period of Peter's confession: that 'there be those standing here who shall not taste death until they have seen the Son of man coming in his glory.'

"Then what were the purposes of the lesson to you, as an individual, from the transfiguration, some six or eight days later—that event upon the mountain, witnessed by Peter and James and John—when the glory of the Lord became visible and Moses and Elias appeared?

"Did Moses and Elias give strength to him or gain strength from him? This is an important lesson in thy experience.

"It is within that there is the kingdom of heaven! The kingdom of God is without, but is manifested in how it is reacting upon thee—by the manner in which ye mete to thy associates day by day that concept of that which rises within!

"Not that the light, then, is other than to bring encouragement. And ye may indeed say, then, even as they, 'Let us make here a tabernacle.' What, indeed, is thy tabernacle? It is thy body, thy mind, thy soul! Present them, therefore, as things holy, acceptable unto Him who is the giver of all good and perfect gifts!"

Further information was given by Cayce concerning this experience, the transfiguration of Jesus and the appearance of Moses and Elijah (or Elias) in answer to a question concerning the communion of saints. "What saw they [Peter, James and John]?" Cayce asks. "A glorified body? The glory of the body brought what? Communion of saints! For who appeared with him? Moses, that to those present meant a definite undertaking which set them apart from other peoples, which had made for the first association or communication direct with a creative force or God through the activative forces in their experience. And Elijah, or John the Baptist, representing that they, too, would become as messengers to a waiting world, ready, ripe unto the harvest as he had told them. Then this, indeed, was the communion of saints."

As indicated in the Bible, Cayce said, it was hard for those of the Master's followers who saw not his transfiguration upon the mount, to know why they themselves could not heal as heretofore, when he had withdrawn into the mount "that there might be material evidence in the flesh to his faithful three."

"Thus was the power or the might withdrawn," he explained, "and as indicated, fasting and prayer must cast such conditions out."

Yet fasting is often misunderstood. "Get the truth of fasting," Cayce admonishes. "Fasting is not only, as thought by many, the abstaining from food, but the abstaining from all those desires and influences which in thine own consciousness may come between thyself and that ye seek as the Creative Spirit within thy tabernacle."

During that last year of the ministry of the Master in the earth there were continually "those trials, those temptations, those activities and those desires for the ability of those in authority to trap him." So, as John records, "Jesus walked in Galilee, for he would not walk in Jewry, because the Jews sought to kill him." However, he went secretly to Jerusalem for the Feast of Tabernacles, and at about the midst of the feast began to teach in the temple; and it was then, according to John, that the scribes and Pharisees, "tempting him that they might have whereof to accuse him," brought to him the woman taken in adultery.

The information given by Cayce clears up a puzzling question—an apparent discrepancy between the account given by Luke and that given by John. For this woman is generally considered to have been Mary Magdalene— yet this event was during the latter part of Jesus' ministry, while it was during the earlier part, according to Luke, that "Mary called Magdalene, out of whom went seven devils" was among those women who followed him and ministered to him.

According to Cayce, "there were two individual experiences when he was questioned as to the law as related to that given by Moses respecting those taken in adultery," and "the question in each instance were by the different sects of people."

In the latter incident, Cayce says, in which the woman was brought before Jesus in the temple, she had been "taken in the act with the Roman soldiery," and "because of the judgment passed upon that maid according to the law, the peoples of the high priest, or those of the Sanhedrin (led by the Sadducees) declared that he must make a statement.

111

"And he gave, 'Let him that is without sin cast the first stone. Let him that has been guiltless make the first move for fulfilling the letter of the law.'

"And lo, they all went their way. And as he wrote upon the ground: 'Medi, Medici, Cui' (the expression of mercy and not sacrifice) these meant in the experience of those that looked on that which showed the awakening in the heart of the entity of hope, and as the cry came, 'Master, what sayest thou?' the answer came, 'I condemn thee not, Daughter. Go and sin no more.' "

Is it any wonder then, Cayce asks, that those days that followed made for a remolding of this woman? For, though she kept afar, he says, and not until after the persecution of the disciples began "did she venture to come nigh unto those that were classed or called of the household of faith, yet to have had the words direct from the Master of Masters, the Teacher of Teachers, 'I do not condemn thee,' has meant, must mean that which words cannot portray, but only the deeds of the body, the desire of the mind to bring hope, faith in the Lord, that Master who is able to save to the utmost, and who hath given to all, 'My peace I leave with you. My peace I give unto you.' "

During the next few months, according to John, Jesus continued to teach in Jerusalem, and healed a man born blind. Upon one occasion the Jews, angry because he reproved them, attempted to stone him. Shortly thereafter, because of his statement that he was the Son of God, which they considered blasphemy, they attempted again to seize him. He left Judea then and went into Perea, that country beyond Jordan where John had baptized, and remained there until that period when there was the death of Lazarus.

When Jesus came to Bethany, to the tomb of Lazarus, questions arose in the minds of many of those who had come to comfort those bereaved sisters. For they knew of the miracles of healing Jesus had performed, and of the love he had for this family.

Why did the Master delay, when he had been notified of the illness of Lazarus, that brother of Mary and Martha, they must have wondered—as many have questioned, even today. Why did he come only when the dead body had been for four days in the tomb, and the hearts of his loved ones were heavy with grief? Why could not the Master have spared those he loved so well those days of sorrow?

Though Cayce gave no direct answer to this question, his answer to a similar question would apply here as well. "Some might easily ask," he said, "if he were the healer, why was it necessary that Joseph pass away?" And the answer is implied: Did the Master come to be about his work or the Father's work? As individuals, as representatives of the Master, as heirs with him, do we go about our Father's work or our work? There is the variation."

It seems quite likely that the reason was that as was said of the man born blind: "That the works of God should be made manifest," that God might be glorified in the minds and hearts of many. This is implied by Cayce in the following statement:

"While much has been said as to his visits, his friendship with Mary, Martha, Lazarus, we find that much remains to be said as to how that friendship with those brought so much into the hearts of men at that experience [the raising of Lazarus], many who never followed, save as afar."

Cayce's information concerning the experiences of many of those associated with this event furnishes not only additional circumstantial details but also illuminates the effects this experience had upon the lives and consciousness of these individuals. Among these were Ulai, Ruth, the sister of Jesus, and Susane, the daughter of Cleopas.

Ulai, said Cayce, had "come into activity in the heterogeneous or conglomerate thought" brought about by the

113

many various sects and religious beliefs in Palestine in that period. Her father, Archaus, although a member of the orthodox group, was a close adherent to the Essenes' thought. Her mother, Josada, was a close associate of Martha, Mary and Lazarus, therefore presumably associated with the Essene group. Therefore, she was acquainted with the teachings of both the orthodox groups that held to the service in the temple, and the teachings of the Essenes or Carmelites, as they had been known, since this school of thought had been the attempt at a reconstruction of the former activities established by Elijah in Mount Carmel. Then, as apparently happened in so many cases in that time, she became associated with students and exponents of the Roman and Grecian beliefs. So, coming under the influence of all of these, she was greatly confused in her early years, but turned more to the Roman and Grecian beliefs than the others.

Thus, when she was first presented with the teachings of Jesus, the Nazarene, as she had rejected John as a forerunner, "these appeared as mysteries" to Ulai. She became acquainted with the Master's teachings during the time when he visited in Bethany, in the home of her cousins there, and she was apparently much impressed and excited, yet pulled between opposing influences, for, Cayce says, she often grew cold, and again very enthusiastic as to the varying forms of activities.

Then, when Mary returned, after the conversion and the casting out of the demons, Ulai was more confused than ever. For, to her—"How *could* anyone who had been such a person, or who had disregarded persons except for the material gains, become an honored one among these, or in association with a household of ones such as Lazarus and Martha?"

For Lazarus, "the friend, the companion of those who loved his name, who loved his manner, his way [that of the Master], held an honored position. Though he was hated by many people, he "set about to accomplish, under

114

the various forces of the time, the period, the place, the circumstances, that which few accomplished that bore the name of those that were in the position of leaders of the people during the time." Cayce didn't say just what was the position held by Lazarus, nor the exact nature of what he accomplished as one who would be helpful to his own people, yet much is implied in the statement that "many were the calls that were made upon Lazarus, either by those in places of power, or those that were oppressed by those in power, or by those that would come and seek counsel on account of the position occupied by him."

So, though Lazarus and his sisters were closely associated with the Master in their home, the cousin, Ulai, because of Mary, "withheld self from such associations until there were the periods in which Lazarus was ill of a fever —what today would be called the slow fever, or typhoid— and there was the eventual death." Then Ulai was among "those of the mourners—not the hired mourners, but as a relative of the family—and came in contact again with Mary and Martha during those periods of the Master's expressions at the grave of Lazarus." And to Ulai, that which is expressed in the shortest verse recorded in Holy Writ was that to which she responded deepest within self.

"For," said Cayce, "with that concept of how he, the friend, wept with those of his friends in the face of criticism, in the company of the great and near great, there came a conviction to Ulai that changed her whole concept as to the purposes, as to the whys and wherefores of that which had taken place in the mind and heart of Mary; also as to why and how that Martha and Lazarus had again accepted this sister into their home and company."

Martha, the wife of Nicodemus, held in the beginning an attitude similar to that of Ulai as to the return of Mary to the home of her brother and sister. Although she had become a most helpful influence in the lives and activities of the Holy Women, in this one area, for a time, there was a lack of cooperation. "The only differences which arose," Cayce said, "were with Martha and Mary in the household of Lazarus. Because of conditions there from which Mary had returned, from the houses which were a portion of her activity in various cities, questions as to morality arose. And yet, after there were the healings, or after it was discovered how there were even changes then and there, we find there was a greater working together with the activities of Mary and Martha and Lazarus."

Thelda, one of the hired mourners at the death of Lazarus, "became a believer through seeing the activities, experiencing the influence of the Master's life on the friends, associates and acquaintances of the group there," and was "henceforth known as one of the Holy Women."

Susane, the friend of Ruth, was also present in Bethany when Lazarus was raised from the grave. "For with those changes that came about by the shifting of the ministry of the Master to the area closer about Jerusalem, Susane had joined with those activities at Bethany," becoming a neighbor to Mary and Martha and Lazarus. And what was the thought of this girl who had once followed after Judas in the desire for material benefits through the earthly kingship of the Messiah? "The thought," said Cayce, "that inspires each soul to determine within self to give itself in service to that ideal, that principle in him."

Ruth, the sister of Jesus, had traveled to Bethany in an effort to ascertain the truth of those things told concerning her brother, the experiences in Bethlehem, the activities of friends at Bethany. And she witnessed the raising of Lazarus there, as did also the companion, Philoas, who had accompanied her to Bethany. This experience, said Cayce, "brought about a change which made for a new life, a new understanding, a new conception of the manifestations of the Creative Force, or God, among the children of men."

For, as expressed by Cayce, "as experienced by those who stood about the grave of him, the brother of those whom the Lord loved—when he spoke, death itself gave up that it had claimed, even though, as the sister had warned, there had not been the embalming as had been the purposes of many. Instantly the activity brought life. For he is life; he is health; he is beauty. He is—not was, not will be, but is."

There were "great turmoils about those of the city of Bethany," said Cayce, "when Lazarus was raised from the grave, when those of the followers, those of the sisters —Martha and Mary—made preparations for the supper after the resurrection or the bringing to life of the brother." Susane, then, taking part in those activities, "saw the fears created by those in authority who questioned Susane and the parents and those about the feast."

Those fears created by the questioning is not surprising. According to the Bible, both the life of Jesus and that of Lazarus were in danger. For the chief priests and the Pharisees counseled together, alarmed lest the miracles Jesus performed should cause all the people to follow after him and cause the Romans to take away their authority and perhaps even destroy their nation. So they plotted together to put him to death, as a little later they plotted also against the life of Lazarus, since it was because of him that many of the Jews believed in Jesus.

Jesus and his disciples, aware of course of this danger, withdrew to Ephraim, a city near the wilderness, and later went again into the area beyond Jordan. There the little children were brought to him that he might bless them, and some of these, Cayce said, gained healing abilities from that experience. There also the young ruler came to him and questioned him.

Nicholas was the name, according to a reading given by Cayce, of the rich young ruler who asked, "How may I have eternal life? What lack I yet?" He was, said Cayce, "that one about whom much speculation has been in the minds of many, over what is written there in the records, concerning which many a verbose orator has

117

proclaimed much about which he knew so little." For, though the young ruler, went away sorrowing, "remember another line, 'The Master loved the young man.' He whom the Master has favored in mind or in purpose may count his soul indeed fortunate. Remember one of those eternal laws, 'He hath not willed that any soul should perish.' "

" 'Sell that thou hast and come and follow me," Jesus said. And Nicholas, said Cayce, "did just that. He came later and followed."

Cayce implies that it was he who "prompted Nicodemus to seek the Lord," and prompted "those that cared for the body when it was placed in a new tomb."

"And much might be said," Cayce said in another reading, referring to this rich young ruler, "as to the helpful forces that came into the lives and experiences of many, owing to the activities of that young man during the times of the persecutions of the disciples."

Soon after these incidents in Perea, the land beyond the Jordan, there came the period when the feast of the Passover was drawing near, and Jesus said to his disciples, "Behold, we go up to Jerusalem."

So, although the disciples were fearful, there began that journey which had its end at Calvary.

"In those days preceding the entry into Jerusalem," said Cayce, "we find those periods of much disturbance among the disciples who were of Galilee and those who were of the Judean ministry. These were in disputation as to what was to take place when he, Jesus, was to go to Jerusalem.

"Yet he chose to go, entering through the period of rest at Bethany with Mary, Martha and Lazarus, and from there the triumphal entry, and the message that was given to those throngs gathered there."

CHAPTER SEVEN

THE HOLY WEEK

In those days when the feast of the Passover was at hand, according to Cayce, "there were those gatherings from all the lands nigh to the Galilean, the Phoenician or Syro-Phoenician, Tyre and Sidon; and all the peoples of the faith of the Jews had come as one for the days that were counted as holy."

Many of these travelers as well as some residents of the area witnessed the entrance of Jesus into Jerusalem, the triumphal entry recorded in all the gospels. Cayce relates the experience of some of these, the attitudes, the effects of this experience.

Phoebe, he said, "was among the Syro-Phoenician people that had heard, through the journeys into the land, of the activity of the individual, or the man [Jesus] in that land; and she came with many and with those of the lands adjoining same, for that period when there was to be either the establishing of the material kingdom by that man, or there were to be the understandings of what those teachings were to bring into the experience of others." She was present "when there was the procession, or the triumphal entry into Jerusalem, the crowd of people, the throngs, mostly of women and children."

Sylvia, from the land of Tyre and Sidon, who had become acquainted with "that as had been told of the visit of that teacher" from Galilee to her own country, had come shortly prior to this time to the country near to Jerusalem and "made overtures not to the Holy Women, but rather to those who had been as companions to him in Bethany, in Bethsaida, in Bethlehem and Capernaum, and questioned them."

119

The confusion as to those reports, Cayce said, brought confusion to Sylvia. "But when the eyes of the Master, as he passed by on the road or way to the city on that day of days, were seen by Sylvia, when he gave that if it were not for the cry of the peoples the very hills and mountains would cry out, 'Hosanna, Glory in the Highest, for the Prince of Peace comes to make those decisions whereunto man again has his closer, closer association with his Maker,' then Sylvia understood; then she realized that man, as man, may be far from God, but man as a god and acting godly may be close to the divine."

Sarapha, too, was in that position as to have a part in that great experience. For the inn where she "made for those feelings in the experience of each and every traveler that there was a care and a thought for their own or their individual appurtenances for rest and harmony and beauty," was on the road where the Master passed on that day. And she was "among that mighty throng that cried, 'Hosanna to the Highest—the King cometh!' And there again she met those disappointments when that mighty force, that glorious creature, that mighty man among men was not proclaimed king." She was disappointed that he seemed to exert so little of "that necessary material application of a glorious power and might" which had, she knew, been demonstrated "over those things in man's experience of sickness, of doubt, of fear." For many of those who had been healed were known to her. She had been especially close to that one, Bartimaeus, who only lately had had his sight restored by the Master. Bartimaeus, "strong in body, yet lacking in sight, a worker in those things pertaining to the metals" had often rested by the way close to the wayside inn where Sarapha lived.

One of the individuals present on that occasion was later, according to Cayce, very important in the affairs and activities of the Christian movement, or that called the early church, and those who were its leaders. This was a young girl named Mariaerh.

120

Mariaerh "grew up in the hill country of Judea, nigh unto those places where Elizabeth and Zacharias had lived—Zacharias becoming as it were the first of the martyrs, Elizabeth remaining in the land of the hill country."

There Mariaerh was brought up and taught, and she "was acquainted in her very early years with the visiting of John by the young man, just before his ministry began, who in his return was called Jesus."

Mariaerh's parents "were of the Jewish peoples and those that were disturbed or had been a remnant or a portion of the Galilean peoples." Apparently, Cayce is referring here to that remnant that intermarried with the people of the conquering nation, and became the Samaritans. Since these people did not hold with the Rabbinical interpretation of the law, including the consideration of Jerusalem as the proper place to worship, there had been little of the strictly orthodox Jewish activity in her early experience, and she only came to Jerusalem, Cayce says, "at the age of accountability according to women, in about her fourteenth year, to be recorded, or polled, as to those that were of the marriagable age, or taxable, or for the whole consideration both from the Jewish and the Roman requirements for the poll or taxation."

It was at this period during which the Master, Jesus, made that triumphal entry from Bethany to Jerusalem that Mariaerh made her first visit to this area, when she came with her own parents and Elizabeth and others of the older people from "the little town in the hills to the city of the many strange noises, the many strange lights, the many unusual customs." She became acquainted then "with many of those during those periods that were later called the Holy Women," and for the first time heard of, or became fully acquainted with the happenings in Bethany, or the raising of Lazarus and the activities and influences associated with this event.

So she experienced, witnessed, "not only that triumphal entry, but the humbleness yet the graciousness, the glory, the dignity of the man who, with his disciples, waited among friends that from the material angle sought that he not expose the physical man to danger; and yet, as he preached or as he counseled, he gave that indeed for that purpose came he into the world, and as a man must stand forth for what had been the purpose for his entrance.

"And Mariaerh caught that concept of how each soul must in each experience live as the grain of wheat, as the grain of mustard, as the seeds of every nature, fulfilling that purpose for which it enters into an experience in a sojourn, irrespective of self's individual or personal desires, letting the personality of self be lost in the individuality of the Christ purpose as he so magnificently gave in that way from Bethany to Jerusalem."

During those periods of the last journey into Jerusalem, as indicated by the experiences of these individuals, though many misunderstood, hoping for deliverance not from the bondage to sin but from the material bondage to the power of Rome, yet to some, says Cayce, there came a better understanding of what was being presented to a stiff-necked people—that as touched the hearts, the minds, the lives of those people during that experience.

And to the people of this day, also, are these truths being presented by the spirit of the Son: "These are the days when the paths must be made straight, that, indeed, there may be peace on earth.

"For, even as he gave on that memorable day, if the people do not proclaim him—or if the people had not cried 'Hosanna'—the very rocks, the very trees, the very nature about, would cry out *against* those opportunities lost by the children of men, to proclaim the great day of the Lord."

During the days that followed the entry into Jerusalem, according to accounts in Matthew, Mark and Luke, Jesus taught openly in the temple, answering the many questions asked of him; and although those in authority plotted his death they dared not take him openly for fear of the great crowds that followed him.

In the evenings he withdrew to the Mount of Olives, to the home of those friends in Bethany. And on the way he instructed his disciples concerning those things that must come to pass—his death, his resurrection, and the signs of the coming of the end of the age. One of the statements he made then has brought confusion and questioning to many: "Verily, I say unto you, this generation shall not pass till all these things be fulfilled." Obviously, all these things have not yet come to pass. What then? Must we believe that this prediction was in error? Not if Cayce's explanation can be accepted.

The meaning of this statement, he said, is this: "Those individuals that were in hearing and in keeping of those things presented by the Master in that experience would be in the manifested form in the earth during the periods of fulfillments in the earth of the prophecies spoken of. Not in what is termed the generation of four score and ten years, but the experience of those souls in the earth during those periods when there must shortly come the completing or fulfilling of those things spoken of."

One of these prophecies or predictions made by Jesus at this time was concerning those who should come saying, "I am Christ."

"As had been given," Cayce says, "many have arisen; for, as he gave in the same connection, there were many false prophets, even those that would lead the very elect away.

"There be those who, finding something of the power that is in the material activities of those that would walk in the light, turn same into their own selfish purposes, hence become false prophets, false Christs, and lead many astray. Let's remember, there has been given the manner, the way, to determine as to whether such a prophet is of the Spirit of God or not. They that deny the call of the prophets of old, or the burdens of the world upon the Son, or his death, his resurrection, are not of the Spirit; for, 'As ye have seen him go, so shall he come.' As he overcame the world through the birth, as one born in due season, through those varied periods when necessity and the demands of the Sons of God brought forth those leaders in their proper places, so he is that one that is given power made manifest in the consciousness of him and his power in the earth; hence we may see how the consciousness of his presence may be misconstrued when turned to selfish motives. Know that even as the powers of evil are loosed for the correcting of many, so are the glories of him made manifest in the hearts and lives of many."

According to the Gospels another warning, one which seems quite similar to the one explained above, was given by Jesus: "Then if any man shall say unto you, 'Lo, here is Christ, or there,' believe it not . . . For as the lightning cometh out of the east and shineth even unto the west, so shall also be the coming of the Son of man." A rather different explanation to this was implied by Cayce as he referred to the "contentions arising in that called in the present 'denominationalism,' and each one crying, 'Lo, here is Christ—Lo, this is the manner of approach—Lo, unless ye do this or that ye have no part in Him.'

He, the Christ, the Son, said Cayce, was manifested in all those forms of philosophy or religious thought that taught God was one, through the association with, in meditation or spirit, that one guiding same; "and all those things that have been added are much in the same manner as that added by Judaism. These have all been added to much from that given by Jesus in his walk in Galilee, in Judea. In all of these there is the same impelling spirit.

"What individuals have done, do do, to the principles or the spirit, in turning this aside to meet their own im-

124

mediate needs in material planes or places has made for that which becomes an outstanding thing, as a moralist or the head of any independent religious force or power; for, as has been given, 'Know, O Israel, the Lord thy God is One!'—whether this is directing one of the Confucius thought, Brahman thought, Buddha thought, Mohammedan thought—These are as teachers or representatives, or to make more of a distinct charge, that given by the apostle of the gentiles: 'I hear there are divisions among you. Some say, I am of Paul, another, I am of Apollo, another, I am of Cephas. Paul may minister, Apollo may have watered, but it is God that gives the increase.'

"The spirit of the Creative Force, and as such the Son, represented in the spirit that made manifest in the earth. Not as only one, but as the *only* one; for as he gave, 'He that climbs up another way is a thief and a robber.'

"As the spirit of the Master, the spirit of the Son was manifested, each in their respective sphere. As it is today, and as it was of yore—God calls on man everywhere to seek His face, through that channel that may be blessed by the *spirit* of the Son, in whatsoever sphere this may take its form. Because there are contentions, because there is the lack of giving and taking as to other's thought, does not change God's attitude one whit; Neither does it make one above another. There is only one Master—the others are acting in the capacity of the thought that was given through that same power, that "In the last days He has spoken to us through the Son, as one born out of due season.'

" 'He that loves me will keep my commandments.' What are the commandments? 'Thou shalt have no other Gods before me' and 'Love thy neighbor as thyself'; in this is builded the whole law and gospel of every age that has said, 'There is one God.' "

The next period concerning which we are given information by Cayce is that in the upper chamber with the disciples. This, Cayce said, was in the home of John's father, Zebedee. "See what they have for supper," he remarked. "Boiled fish, rice with leeks, wine and loaf."

This statement, if not considered more carefully, might cast some doubt in the minds of some as to the validity of the information, yet if it is true it has considerable significance, giving further evidence upon a point questioned by Bible scholars. For this supper is generally considered to have been the Passover feast, and certainly this is not the food which would be eaten at the Passover. For the lamb killed in the afternoon on the preceding day—the day of preparation—was the main item of the menu.

Yet there is some question as to whether this last supper of Jesus with his disciples was indeed the Passover feast. There are discrepancies between the account of John and that of the other gospel writers, John stating that this was before the Passover. John's account of the trial before Pilate, moreover, indicates clearly that the Passover had not been eaten at that time. The other gospel writers seem to indicate that this was the Passover feast, yet a careful study of the events of this same day, as recorded in these other gospels, also show considerable evidence that this day, beginning at sundown as was the custom of the Jews, must not have been the day of the feast itself, but rather the day of preparation. That both the disciples of Jesus and the mob carried weapons, that the Sanhedrin met to try and to condemn Jesus, the High priest tearing his robe in protest against blasphemy, the execution of Jesus and the preparation for burial—all these would have been in violation of the law or custom for the day of the Passover feast.

It might be asked, what makes this a question of importance, or what is its significance? It was on the day of preparation, the day before the eating of the Passover, that the lamb had been slain whose blood, upon the lintels and the doorposts of the children of Israel in Egypt, caused the angel of death to pass over these homes. Thus it becomes more significant, more meaningful if it were upon this day that the Lamb of God was to be slain, "that the Angel of Death," as Cayce expressed it, "that influence that may, that does separate man from Life itself, might pass over all who partake of that sacrifice."

Cayce gives a vivid description of the Master and some of his disciples at the time of this last supper, as well as some of the details of the event:

"The Master's hair is most red, inclined to be curly in portions. Yet he is not feminine nor weak, but strong with heavy piercing eyes that are blue or steel-gray. His weight would be at least a hundred and seventy pounds. He has long tapering fingers. The nails are well kept, with a long nail though on the left little finger. He is merry, even in the hour of trial; he jokes, even in the moment of betrayal. The whole robe of the Master is not white but pearl gray, all combined in one, the gift of Nicodemus to the Lord.

"The better looking of the twelve is, of course, Judas, while the younger is John with oval face, dark hair, smooth face, the only one with short hair.

"Peter, the rough and ready, has a very short beard— rough and not altogether clean. Andrew's is just the opposite—very sparse but inclined to be long more on the side and under the chin, long on the upper lip.

"Andrew's robe was always near gray, or black, while his clouts or breeches were striped. Those of Philip and Bartholomew were red and brown.

"The sack is empty. Judas departs. The last is given of the wine and loaf.

"The Master lays aside his robe which is all of one piece. He girds the towel about his waist which is dressed with linen that is blue and white. He rolls back the folds and kneels, first before John, then James, then to Peter who refuses. The basin used is without handle and is made of wood. The water is from the firkins that are in the wide-mouthed shibboleths that stand in the house of John's father, Zebedee.

"Now comes the dissertation as to 'He that would be the greatest should be the servant of all.' " For, said Cayce, "though he were their leader, their prophet, their Lord, their Master, he signified—through the humbleness of the act, the washing of their feet—the attitude to which each would come if he would know that true relationship with his God, with his fellow man."

"There is little seen in the faces of the eleven about him, as they leave the upper chamber, of that fear that was created by the leaving of Judas; but rather that as experienced in the heart and mind of all when he gave, "My peace I leave with you . . . Let not your hearts be troubled; in my Father's house are many mansions. . . . I am the Way, the Truth and the Life."

How much controversy, how much bigotry has been caused by the misunderstanding, the lack of understanding of that which, according to Cayce is the true meaning of this statement of the Master! For this explanation is one which may have a constructive, rather than a separative influence in the lives of men.

"How came the Son of man the Way that leads to perfection in heaven and in earth? In overcoming the forces in nature and earth by giving self for others; hence, becoming the Savior of others, becomes the Son and one with the Father.

"That which has been given may be used to illustrate the difference that may be felt by a soul that has become aware of itself as the Christ; or as Jesus, the man, became aware of the Spirit of the Father through those experiences of the man as he 'went about doing good,' and at those periods when there was received those acknowledgments of the Father that he was the one who could, would, through those activities, become the Savior of man. First as 'in whom I am well pleased,' then as 'This is my son; hear ye him.'

128

Latest U.S. Government
tests of all cigarettes
show True is
lower in both
tar and nicotine
than 99% of all other
cigarettes sold.

Think about it.
Shouldn't your next cigarette be True?

Latest U.S. Government
tests of all menthol
cigarettes show
True is lower
in both tar and
nicotine than 99% of
all other menthols sold.

Think about it.
Shouldn't your next cigarette be True?

"In the overcoming, then, he is the Way, the manner in which individuals may become aware of their souls that are in accord with that as may be one with the spirit of truth; for corruption inherits not eternal life. The Spirit is the true life. Then as individuals become aware of that ability in him to be the Way, so they become as the door, as representatives, as agents, as those that present the Way; and the door is opened; not to the man, but to the spirit of self that bears witness with the spirit of truth through him that overcame the world, thus putting the world under his feet."

"In considering that which materially passed through the mind of the Master," Cayce says, "and those experiences leading to the way of the Cross—the decisive point in Perea was the more trying even than the trial; and then those periods of taking leave after the establishing of the emblems of his body and blood, as a ritual for those who would honor and bring to remembrance those experiences through which each soul passes in putting on the whole armor of the Christ.

"Those periods in the garden, these become that in which the great trial is shown, and the seeming indifference, and the feeling of loss of one in whom trust and hope had been given, and the fulfilling of all that had been in the purpose and the desire in the entrance into the world."

The betrayal of the Master by Judas, Cayce said, was because of the desire of the man to force him to assert himself as king, and bring in his kingdom then. Apparently, in spite of all the Master's teaching, Judas never understood the nature of the mission of the Master or his kingdom.

"The trial—this was not with the pangs of pain as so oft indicated, but rather glorying in the opportunity of taking upon self that which would right man's relationship to the Father, in that man, through his free will, had brought sin into the activities of the children of God; here His Son was bringing redemption through the shedding of blood that they might be free.

"Here the law of love, of causation, of mercy, of justice, of all that makes for self becoming in the at-onement relationship, becomes the activity of him that is free indeed. Thus in the hour of sacrifice, material, mental and spiritual relationships are attained and considered in his every word."

As recorded in the gospels, after his arrest Jesus was taken, bound, to the palace of the high priest, Caiphas, where there were assembled scribes and elders and other high priests. Apparently, this was an informal hearing before those who were plotting against him, and when it was morning the Sanhedrin convened for a more formal trial. Although there were many false witnesses, no two agreed on any of those things of which he was falsely accused. Therefore, of this alone he stood condemned—that he said he was the Son of God! Nevertheless, when he was brought before Pilate, the Roman Governor, "there were the claims made," said Cayce, "by those in authority among the Jews that there had been a neglect to pay tribute, or that there had been first that attempt upon the part of those that were as the followers of same to prevent the tax, the levies, to be paid. This was the manner of presentation, rather than so much of that ye have recorded in Holy Writ."

Although it may appear here that Cayce is in disagreement with all the gospel writers, by "so much" he apparently refers rather to the majority. Luke's account states essentially the same as Cayce, that he was accused of "forbidding to give tribute to Caesar."

Matthew relates how Pilate, during the trial of Jesus, was admonished by his wife: "Have nothing to do with this just man, for I have suffered many things in a dream because of him." It might be wondered how much Pilate's wife knew about Jesus. According to Cayce, she was well aware of him and his activities.

It would seem probable that she had heard of him through Agatha, a Galilean woman, who was "an instructress, a teacher in the garrisons of the Roman people, to interpret for the wives, the companions of the Romans the customs of the Samaritans and the Galilean peoples and their relationships with the Jewish portion." For Agatha, was, said Cayce, "a very close associate" of the wife of Pontius Pilate, and was very outspoken as to the acceptance of the various teaching of John and later Jesus.

It was not alone through Agatha's reports, however, that the wife of Pilate had a knowledge of the Master, for she had a more direct experience through the activities of her own household. "Romuloan, a companion or guard for Pilate's wife," said Cayce, "brought their afflicted or epileptic son to the Master for healing." It is no wonder that she was disturbed that he might be condemned to death by her own husband, the father of the child!

This healing of the son of the Roman Governor had been witnessed by some of those of the household of Herod Antipas "that made for such a destructive influences in the minds of many as respecting those relationships and activities of the Master." One of these was Eloin, who had also witnessed the healing of blind Bartimaeus. Another was Cleopeo, among the entertainers at the court of Herod.

According to the Gospels, Pilate, with his wife's warning, as well as his own recognition that there was no fault in this man, would have released Jesus. But those in the throng shouted, "Crucify him!" and those who might have spoken in his defense had fled in fear.

So he was condemned, and they led him out to Golgotha, bearing his cross. And, said Cayce, he laughed! "This is what angered them most—he laughed! For he

131

laughed and joked often with his disciples, even on the way to the cross."

When Jesus had borne his cross up Mount Calvary to that placed called Golgotha, and there had been nailed to the cross, the gospels relate, the soldiers divided his garments among them and cast lots for his robe. This robe, according to Cayce, had been made by Martha, the wife of Nicodemus, as a gift to the Master.

For when the message had been given out that Martha's older sister, the mother of Peter's wife, had been healed from a terrible fever by this man Jesus, this brought about great changes in Nicodemus; and Martha began weaving the robe. Since Nicodemus and Martha were associated "with the temple and the service of the high priest," this influenced the pattern or style of the robe which "became a part of the equipment the Master had."

Cayce gives a detailed description of this robe. "In color it was not as the robe of the priest,"* but pearl gray, "woven in one piece with the hole in the top through which the head was to be placed, and then over the body, so that with cords it was bound about the waist." The selvage was "woven around the neck, as well as that upon the edge, as over the shoulder and to the bottom portion of the robe; no belts, no pomegranates (as upon the robe of the high priest) but those which were woven in such a manner that into the selvage portion of the bottom was woven the Urim and Thummin. These were as a balance in which judgments were passed by the priest; but [in the robe of the Master] these were woven, not placed upon the top of the robe (as they were in the robe of the priest.) Neither were there jewels set in the robe."

This robe Nicodemus had presented to the Master, Jesus, after the raising of the son of the widow of Nain,

* See Exodus 28:31-34 for a description of the robe of the high priest.

132

who was a relative of Nicodemus. And this was the robe for which the soldiers now cast lots.

Martha was among the Holy Women and the relatives and disciples of the Master at the foot of the cross, "one of those upon the right hand of Mary, the mother of Jesus."

Ulai, who from the experience of the raising of Lazarus had been "among those seeking to know something of the heart of the mother," had "made the journey to notify the mother of that taking place in Jerusalem, missing the triumphal entry." Then, when there was the arrest, Josie had also come to the mother and persuaded her to come to Jerusalem, and the other Mary and Eunice had accompanied them. Many other of the women were there— Mary Magdalene, Sophie, who had been among those who saw that vision on the stairs when the first choice of the maidens was made, and . "those who were of that whole group were among the women at the cross."

As he, the Master, the savior of the world, hung upon the cross, Cayce says, "he called to those that he loved, and remembered not only their spiritual purposes but their material lives. For he committed unto those of his brethren not only the care of the spiritual life of the world, but the material life of those who were of his own flesh, his own blood."

And then, according to the gospels, came the cry, when death was near, "My God, my God, why hast thou forsaken me?" and shortly thereafter, "It is finished, Father into thy hands I commend my spirit." Both the statement, "It is finished," and the question, the anguished cry, are made more understandable, given more or a fuller meaning by this extract from the Cayce readings:

"He, from the beginning, was that expressed in 'And God said, Let there be light, and there was light.' Not of the sun but as the Son borne of the Father-God. Thus the continuity of life itself. For without him, without light, was not anything made that was made; this fact

133

conceived, this truth lived in the daily life will put away doubt and fear of every nature. For, 'the earth is the Lord's and the fullness thereof'—'the silver and the gold are His, and the cattle on a thousand hills.'

"Yet in the beginning of man's separation from God, the beginning of the labor of redemption, he said as he showed the way, as he fulfilled in giving his life, 'In the day ye eat thereof ye shall surely die.'

"Yet the temptor said, 'Not surely die, for it may be put off;' and it was—six hundred years—and yet death came, the pangs of the loss of self.

"Then on that day when the voice was raised on the cross, he said, 'Father, why—why the way of the cross?' This is indeed the pattern that is interpreted in 'I perceive that the heart of man is to do evil—the spirit is willing, the flesh is weak.' Not only was he dead in body, but the soul was separated from that body. As all phases of man in the earth are made manifest, the physical body, the mental body, the soul body, become as each dependent upon their own experience. Is it any wonder that the man cried, 'My God, my God, why hast thou forsaken me?'

"Each man comes to stand, as he, before that throne of the Maker, with the deeds that have been done in the body, in the mind, presenting the body spiritual before the throne of mercy, before the throne of the Maker, the Creator, God."

Though this may have been, probably was, the first cross, the first literal crucifixion in the experience of this entity we know as Jesus, in the figurative sense, Cayce tells us, this was not so. "In the beginning," he says, "he was the Son—make the Son—those of the Sons that went astray; and through the varying activities overcame the world through the experiences, bearing the cross in each and every experience, reaching the final cross with all power, all knowledge in having overcome the world, and of himself accepted the cross. Hence doing away with that often termed karma, that must be met by all. The immutable law of cause and effect is, as evidence in the world today, in the material, the mental and the spiritual world; but he—in overcoming the world, the law—became the law. The law, then, becomes as the schoolmaster, or the school of training, and we who have named the Name then, are no longer under the law as law, but under mercy as in him; for in him—and with the desires—may there be made the coordination of all things."

Thus there was accomplished, there was finished upon the cross that sacrifice expressed in the Revelation as "the Lamb slain from the foundation of the world." Why "from the foundation of the world?"

"If this is taken in conjunction with many another expression of the Master," said Cayce, "it may be the more easily comprehended in the intellectual activities of those who seek to experience same.

"As the Master gave, 'Before Abraham was, I am—before the worlds were, I am.' Hence, when there came the necessity in the realm of the spiritual home for the coming of the Lamb into the earth for its redemption, the Truth, the Light, the offering was made. Hence the expression, as given by John. For, as has been given, the thought, the mind is the builder.

"Then as each soul builds for that it, as a soul, is to act, whether in mind or in body, the soul mind is already in the throes of the influences necessary. Then when we comprehend, we realize there is no time, no space, and that the divinity of the man, Jesus, was perfect in his own activity in the earth, for it was offered even from the first."

When the soldiers saw that Jesus was dead, according to the Gospel of John, one of them thrust a spear into his side, "and forthwith came there out blood and water," thus fulfilling the law as stated in the book of Hebrews, "without the shedding of blood there is no remission of sins."

"Hence," said Cayce, "his blood was shed as the sacrifice of the just for the unjust, that ye may all stand in the same light with the Father. For 'without the shedding of blood there is not remission of sins' was given in the beginning of man's concept of making atonement for the wrongs done self in relationship to the Creative Forces.

"For the error that man makes is the more oft against himself, making for the breaking of the law as related to Divine influence in the experience. For love is law—law is love in its essence. And with the breaking of the law is the making of the necessity for atonement and forgiveness, in that which may take away error to, or what has been brought in, the experience of the individual.

"Hence, the shedding of the blood in the man, Jesus, made for the atoning for all men, through making himself in at-onement with the law and with love. For through love was brought the desire to make self and his brother in at-onement. Hence, in the atoning, or shedding of the blood, comes the redemption for men, through that which may make for his, man's at-onement with him.

"At-onement may be given even as atonement. At-onement, then, is making self's will one with the Creative Forces that may become the impelling influence in thought, in mind, that is the builder to every act of a physical, mental, or material body.

"Though man be far afield, then, though he may have erred, there is established that which makes for a closer, closer walk with Him through that one who experienced all those turmoils, strifes, desires, urges that may be the lot of man in the earth. Yet he put on flesh, made himself as naught, even as was promised throughout to those who walked and talked with God.

"Then as ye meditate upon the meaning of the crucifixion of this man of God—know that the way is open to thee to approach the throne of God; not as an excuse, not as a justification, but rather in love, in harmony, in that which brings hope for a sin-sick world.

"For this was, is, the fulfillment of promise, the fulfillment of law, the fulfillment of man's estate. Else why did he put on flesh and come into the earth in the form of man, but to be one with the Father to show to man his, man's, divinity, man's relationship to the Maker, to show to man that indeed the Father meant it when he said, 'If ye call I will hear.' "

"Then, though he was the first of man, the first of the Sons of God in spirit, in flesh, it became necessary that he fulfill all those associations, those connections that were to wipe away in the experience of man that which separates him from his Maker."

"Have any among you ever taken thought," asks Cayce in another reading, "as to what was the condition of the world when he made intercession in the world for you? Would, could, life have remained in the earth without his having given his life for those who were seeking to know God? No! For in those days it was necessary that the wickedness which had risen as a stench before the throne of God be eliminated from material manifestation. He in that day offered himself that ye, here, now, might know the love the Father hath for the children of men!"

According to the gospels, when the evening of that day of sorrow had come, the body of the Master was prepared for burial according to the customs of the day, and laid in the tomb—the unused tomb of Joseph of Arimathea. These customs called for the body to be wrapped in linen cloths with spices, with a separate cloth or napkin about the head.

According to Cayce, the wrappings for the last annointing of the body of the Holy One were prepared by Andra, that daughter of Elois who had been one of the companions of Mary in the temple—"rather the wrappings than the spices, for Josie and Mary Magdalene and Mary the mother of the Lord prepared these." For "is it any

137

wonder," Cayce asks, "that when there were those preparations of the body for burial, Josie was chief among those who brought the spices, the ointments that were to consecrate the preparations of this body for which she had cared through those early periods of his experience in the earth?"

"The napkins that were about his head with those seals that were later made as raised figures" were among the wrappings that Andra prepared. The figures on these seals were "the seals of the Holy One, as the seals of the son of David: the pear with the bell, with the pomegranates on either side."

When the body of Jesus had been placed in the tomb, Cayce says, the mother, Mary, did not immediately go to the house of John, but rather to that of Ulai, the cousin of Mary, Martha and Lazarus, for it was nearby.

The Holy Women "in that period acted as mourners for Mary." Among these was Sarapha, who "aided in sustaining those of the household that were beginning to feel that possibly the mother, Mary, had misjudged. Yet Sarapha knew from her own experience, had not forgotten that choir before the celestial throne that sang, "Glory in the highest—Peace—Peace on earth, to all men of good will."

CHAPTER EIGHT

THE RESURRECTION AND ASCENSION

"The period of the resurrection—Here we have that in which *all* may glory. For without the fact of his overcoming death, the whole of the experience would have been as naught."

It was to Mary Magdalene, Cayce says, that "the Master first appeared upon the resurrection morn." Although there are some discrepancies in the various Gospel accounts of the experience of the women at the tomb, there is general agreement on this point; also that Mary had been among those who first discovered that the tomb was empty, the stone rolled away.

The effect which his death had had upon this disciple, this friend, Cayce said, is indicated by the fact that when she first saw the Master, "as visioned by that which is read, she thought he was the gardener. This indicated all the hopelessness, all the sorrow that is possible to be indicated in hopelessness."

"Then came they of his brethren, with the faithful women, those that loved his mother, those that were her companions in sorrow, those that were making preparations that the law might be kept, that even there might not be a desecration of the ground about his tomb. They too, of his friends, his loved ones, his brethren, saw the angels.

"How, why took they on form? That there might be implanted into their souls and hearts that fulfillment of those promises.

"For what meaneth the story of the Christ, of the man, Jesus, that walked in Galilee, without that resurrection morn?

"What is the meaning of the resurrection? Is it not fitting that to those in that land it came at that particular season when life, in its manifestations was being demonstrated in the material things about each soul? For the breaking forth from the tomb is exemplified in the bulb of the tree of nature itself breaking forth from the sleep, that it may rise as he with healing in its very life, to bring all phases of man's experience to his consciousness— that indeed became then the fulfilling of the law."

The appearance of Jesus to two of the disciples on the road to Emmaus and to those who were assembled together at Jerusalem is briefly recorded in the Gospels. Piecing together information given by Cayce in the life readings of some of the individuals said to have been associated with these events gives additional and interesting details.

During the actual period of the crucifixion, according to Cayce, the Roman, Philoas, was in Rome, or upon the way from Rome to Palestine, arriving in Palestine just the day after the Crucifixion. With him was Ruth, the sister of Jesus, for shortly before the last journey of Jesus into Jerusalem Ruth and Philoas had been married. Jesus had attended that wedding also, and blessed them. While Philoas had been in Rome the arrest, the trial, the crucifixion had come about. Deeply disturbed by the reports, Philoas and Ruth returned to those environs of Jerusalem, or Bethany, where those of the family and friends were gathered; and as it was a portion of Philoas' government work to inspect the activities about Emmaus, the journey from Jerusalem to Emmaus upon the first day of the week became then a natural thing. He accompanied two of the disciples of the Master—one, Cleopas, the tax collector, the father of Susanne; the other, one close to a brother-in-law of Pilate, and of those same provinces in the Grecian rule that were under the Roman authorities, Luke, the beloved physician.

"As there had been created in the heart and mind of Philoas, there was, as has ever been the promise, 'Draw nigh to me, and I, thy Lord, will draw nigh to thee.' And he came, and walked and talked. Yet they knew him not!"

As the crucifixion was still so fresh in their minds, it was not only the topic of conversation of those of his followers that were so bewildered, but of those that had been touched, and information concerning the happenings was still being sought by those in authority. And as the questions arose in the discussion, Philoas inquired not only of the companions but of the Master as to what had been the happenings, what part the Romans, what part the Jews, what part others had taken, and the conditions surrounding all of the phenomena that arose—as to the opening of graves, the rending of the veil of the temple and the like.

Though Philoas knew the Master well, he was not wholly understanding, as the following conversation indicates: "Hast thou heard the happenings of the day? Hast thou known the considerations upon or of this man, both from the religious and the economic standpoint, also the civil experiences of same?"

And only in the breaking of the bread did the consciousness come of that which he answered. For he spoke to them of all that had been prophesied concerning himself. Then, as they sat at meat in the inn, as he brake the bread, there came the knowledge that they spoke with the Master. Thus Philoas was again physically in association, in touch with the influence of the Master, Jesus, who became the Christ in the life lived. And thus he, Philoas, broke bread with Life itself!

When the Master had left them, the disciples immediately returned to the environs of Jerusalem, to Bethany, where the disciples were gathered in the home of Martha and Mary. For with the death and separation of the Master from the disciples, this became for the time rather the center for most of the activities of the disciples.

Even as they spoke together in the upper chamber, relating the appearances—to Mary in the garden, and to the disciples, Cleopas and Luke, upon the road—the Master appeared in their midst, though the doors were closed. And though there was joy, there was also disbelief and fearfulness at this, to them, supernatural appearance, as of a spirit.

But he took food, and ate before them; and he breathed upon them and said unto them, "Receive ye the Holy Ghost," to alleviate the doubt and fear which arose in the minds and hearts of those gathered in that room. As the breath of life was breathed into the body of man, so breathed he that of love and hope into the experience of those who were to become witnesses of him in the material world.

It is not surprising that there was fear among the disciples, confronted with what seemed to them, as indeed it would to us, an unfathomable mystery. Cayce was once asked to explain this mystery of the transmutation of human flesh to flesh divine.

"There is no mystery," Cayce said, "to the transmutation of the body of the Christ. For having attained in the physical consciousness the at-onement with the Father-Mother-God, the completeness was such that with the disintegration of the body, as indicated in the manner in which the shroud, the napkin lay, there was then the taking of the body-physical form. This was the manner. It was not a transmutation as of changing from one to another.

"Just as indicated in the manner in which the body physical entered the upper room with the door closed, not by being a part of the wood through which the body passed, but by forming from the ether waves that were within the room, because of a meeting prepared by faith. For as had been given, 'Tarry ye in Jerusalem, in the upper chamber, until ye be endued with power from on high.'

"As indicated in the spoken word to Mary, in the garden, 'Touch me not, for I have not yet ascended to my Father,' the body (flesh) that formed that seen by the normal or carnal eye of Mary was such that it could not be handled until there was the conscious union with the sources of all power, all force. But afterwards, when there had been the second, third, fourth, and even the sixth meeting, then he said, "Put forth thy hand and touch the nail prints in my hands, my feet. Thrust thy hand into my side, and believe.' This indicated the transformation.

"For, as indicated, when the soul departs from the body (this is not being spoken of the Christ, you see) it has all of the form of the body from which it has passed, yet it is not visible to the carnal mind, unless that mind has been and is attuned to the infinite. Then it appears, in the infinite, as that which may be handled, with all the attributes of the physical being, with the appetites, until these have been accorded to a unit of activity with universal consciousness.

"Just as it was with the Christ body: 'Children, have ye anything here to eat?' This indicated to the disciples, the apostles present, that this was not transmutation, but regeneration, re-creation of the atoms and cells of the body that might, through desire, masticate material things; fish and honey, in the honeycomb, were given."

After that period in which he appeared on several occasions to the apostles and other disciples in Bethany, those apostles returned to Galilee, as they had been bidden by the Master, who told them, "I will meet you there."

Then came that event as recorded, when the seven who were the fishermen of Galilee went fishing upon the sea—Simon Peter, and Andrew, his brother; Phillip of

143

Bethsaida, Nathanial of Cana, Thomas called Didymus, or the twin, and James and John, the sons of Zebedee.

Then, as indicated, when the Master stood by the sea, "the apostles who saw him from the distance could not, in the early morning light, discern who he was. But when he spoke the voice made the impression upon the mind of the beloved disciple such that he spoke, 'It is the Lord!' "

When they had come to shore, and found there a fire prepared upon the earth, with bread and fishes cooked upon the coals, the Master bade them come and eat.

Then came that question to Peter (and to us all it comes) "Lovest thou me, more than these?" And the command, as given, "Feed my sheep! Feed my lambs!"

It has been asked what is the difference, symbolic or practical, between these two, the sheep and the lambs. "Symbolical," Cayce answered. "One represents that of the fold, and the other that seeking the fold. The sheep represent those that know of, and know the way. The lambs represent those that seek, that would know, that would find the way, that would come if shown the tenderness expressed in 'The good shepherd feedeth the sheep; he tendeth the lambs.'

"To *all* it may be as this: The time draweth near, the time is at hand when there is more and more seeking for the light and understanding. Let each, then, in your own way, in that which seemeth good in the light of that which has been presented thee, from day to day so manifest that love that has been showered on thee, . . . so live thine own life that it may be an example to those that seek. . . . And let thy spirit bear witness in the things thy body does day by day that the Lord is in his holy temple, and the rod has not passed from those that call on His name."

For forty days after the resurrection the Master talked often with his disciples—and not the apostles only, for he

144

appeared to many in Galilee, said Cayce, and there were about five thousand who heard and saw him at one time.

Then the apostles who had been chosen that they might be witnesses unto him in all the earth, in obedience to the command of the Master, returned to Jerusalem, there to wait for the promise of the Father, the power that should come with the baptism of the Holy Ghost. And there, near Jerusalem, upon the mount of Olives, he departed from them.

"Five hundred beheld him as he entered into glory," Cayce said; "and saw the angels and heard their announcement of the event that must one day come to pass —and will—only to those who believe and have faith, who look for and expect to see him as he is."

This message, this announcement by the angels, "He shall come again as ye have seen him go," is one which has been the source of much disagreement, much debate, much questioning. Is this "second coming" only to be in a figurative sense, the coming of the Christ Spirit, or the awakening to each individual soul? Or may we expect this to be fulfilled in a literal way and manner, the appearance of the entity, Jesus, in a material or flesh body? Cayce gives a definite answer:

"Then, again he may come in body to claim his own." And "Ye, too, may minister in those days when he will come in flesh, in the earth, to call his own by name."

An even more definite statement on the manner or nature of his coming is given in the following statement by Cayce:

"For he shall come as ye have seen him go, in the body he occupied in Galilee, the body that he formed, that was crucified on the cross, that rose from the tomb, that walked by the sea, that appeared to Simon, that appeared to Phillip, that appeared to John."

It has been asked whether he, Jesus the Christ, is now manifesting on the earth plane in another body.

"All power in heaven, in earth," said Cayce, "is given

145

to him who overcame. Hence, he is of himself in space, in the force that impels through faith, through belief, in the individual entity, as a spirit entity. Hence not in a body in the earth, but may come at will to him who wills to be one with, and acts in love to make same possible.

"Is he abroad today in the earth? Yea, in those that cry unto him from every corner; for He, the Father, hath not suffered his soul to see corruption; neither hath it taken hold on those things that make the soul afraid. For he *is* the Son of Light, of God, and is holy before Him. And he comes again in the hearts and minds of those that seek to know his ways."

"When? How soon?" has been the constant cry even from the time of the apostles.

"The time no one knows," said Cayce. "Even as he gave, not even the Son, himself; only the Father. Not until his enemies—and the earth—are wholly in subjection to his will, his powers.

"How soon? When those that are his have made the way clear, passable for him to come."

Yet it would seem, if Cayce is correct, that the fulfillment of that promise is not far off. "That as has been promised through the prophets of old," he said, "the time and half time, has been and is being fulfilled in this day and generation, and soon there will again appear in the earth that one through whom many will be called to meet those that are preparing the way for his day in the earth. The Lord then will come, 'even as ye have seen him go.' "

PART TWO

THE EARLY CHURCH

CHAPTER ONE

THE ESTABLISHING OF THE CHURCH AT JERUSALEM

To the question once asked, "What is the Holy Church?" Cayce replied, "That which makes for the awareness in the heart of the individual.

"An *individual soul* becomes aware that it has taken that Head, that Son, that Man, even, to be the intermediator. *That* is the Church; that is what is spoken of as the Holy Church.

"What readest thou? 'Upon this I will build my church.'

"What church? The Holy Church. Who is the head? That one upon whom the conditions had been set by that question asked. For here ye may find the answer again to many of those questions sought concerning the Spirit, the Church, the Holy Force that manifests by the attuning of the individual, though it may be for a moment. He asked, 'Whom say men that I am?' Then Peter answered, 'Thou are the Christ, the son of the living God!' Then, 'Upon this I will build my church, and the gates of hell shall not prevail against it.' He said to Peter, 'Flesh and blood . . . hath not revealed this unto thee, but my Father which is in heaven.' Heaven? Where? Within the hearts, the minds; the place where Truth is made manifest!"

This explains the reference Cayce sometimes made to "that ye know as the church," or "that now known as the church," when speaking of the organization, the organized activity of the followers of the Christ. The real church, he says, is not a body, not an assembly, not an organization. Over and over he reminds his hearers of these truths: "There is only one Church—even Jesus the Christ!" and "The Church is within self and not in any pope or preacher, or in any building, but within self!"

Nevertheless, even in the larger sense, it may be said that the Church began with the activities at Pentecost following the ascension of the Master; for it was at this time that there began the true awareness of the Christ within, with the pouring out of the Holy Spirit upon the apostles.

After the death and resurrection of Jesus, Cayce tells us, great changes came in the experience of many of the people of Palestine and those who had been in authority among the various groups of the Jewish leaders. "For when there were those reports of his resurrection there were the attempts of the Romans to put aside the questioning of the Jews, but many sought to know. And with the questioning which arose as to the real divinity of Jesus— through and by the experience of those who saw and talked with those who knew the facts concerning what had taken place—the realization and the wonderment of it all dawned upon many of that land; so there was then the humbleness in their activities for the time. And, as the days passed, there were those who were turning more and more to the tenets pertaining to the activities in Jerusalem."

These activities in Jerusalem spoken of here were undoubtedly those that began with the experience at Pente-

148

cost. Before that time, however, there were the important activities of a less public nature.

"During those periods of activity after the crucifixion and resurrection of the Master, and the various meetings that took place, those gathered in the upper room who believed in, were looking for, the promises of the coming of the outpouring of the Holy Spirit."

Those closely associated in Bethany included many besides the apostles. After the return of the aspostles from Galilee and the ascension of Jesus, Mary, his mother, "became a dweller in the home of John, who joined with those in Bethany, hence the associations of Mary the sister of Martha, and John became the closer after this." Mary, the mother of Jesus and the other Mary became bosom friends, and "there was the imbibing of the other Mary and Mary Magdalene of those tenets that were indicated oft by John in the repeating, especially, of the last hours of the Master."

Cleo, the daughter of Andrew, "was among those who were active following the crucifixion in caring for the upper chamber where the disciples and those first followers gathered. Her activities brought blessings to the many, making that chamber as a home, a church, a meeting place, a hopeful experience for those throughout that period."

Others who were said by Cayce to have been closely associated with the apostles and present upon the occasion of the outpouring of the Holy Spirit included Mariaerh, who had come to Jerusalem for the Passover and remained with the Holy Women in and about Bethany; Eunice, who had come with Mary, Josie and the other Mary at the time of the crucifixion; Martha, the wife of Nicodemus; Ulai, in whose home Mary had lived for a time; and Lucius of Cyrene, a kinsman of Luke, with his sister, Nimmuo.

Lucius, though mentioned only briefly in the Bible as a teacher and a companion of Paul, was, according to

Cayce, an important figure in the early church and active in it from its beginning.

Lucius and Nimmuo were among four children in a home that had been of the faith of the Samaritan Jews, said Cayce, but tempered with the teachings of the Grecians and Romans, for they were of Grecian and Roman parentage, and in the early portion of Lucius's experience of the city of Cyrene, later living in Laodicea. The land in which they lived was "under the direct rulership of the Romans, not as in those areas of Palestine where there were the Jewish rulers overseeing, or being superseded by the Jewish religious groups or sects of people. Thus there were those variations of the customs that were a part of those peoples, the influence of both the Grecian and the Roman, according to the tenets of the peoples of the time. . . .

"That particular portion of Asia of which Lucius and Nimmuo were a part had long been under the supervision of the Roman Empire. There had been the attempts of many of those put in authority from the Roman Empire to give every advantage to those who offered promise of being in sympathy with those rulings, or who were in the position to be conducive to making for activities in accord with such rulings. Thus we find that all the family of Lucius and Nimmuo were among those having the greater advantage of the educational facilities of the time."

Yet the associations and influences were not always of the best, for "much of the lewdness of that period had come from the Grecian and Roman peoples that had become a part of that portion of the land," and the area around Laodicea was peopled with those combinations of Grecians, Romans and Jews that had been expelled from portions of Galilee.

"As a developing youth and young man Lucius was known rather as a ne'er-do-well, or one that wandered from pillar to post, or became, as would be termed in present day parlance, a soldier of fortune.

"When there were those activities in and about Jerusalem and Galilee of the ministry of the man Jesus, Lucius came into those environs. Being impelled by the experiences with the followers and the great lessons given by the Teacher, he became as one that was a hanger-on, and of the very intent and purpose that this was to be the time when there was to be a rebellion against the Roman legions, the Romans in authority. And Lucius looked forward to same, acting in the capacity of not an informant, but rather as one attempting to keep in touch with the edicts of the various natures between the political forces in Rome and the political forces among the Jews.

"Lucius was disregarded and questioned by those who were of the Jewish faith who were the close followers of the Master, yet was among those that were sent as those who were to be as teachers, or among the seventy.

"With the arousing, and the demanding that there be more and more of the closer association with the Teacher, Lucius, being of the foreign group, was rejected as one of the apostles, yet was questioned, mostly by John, Peter, Andrew, James, and those who were the closer affiliated or associated with Thomas.

"With those activities that eventually arose in Palestine, and the ministry in the northernmost portions of the land, during the teachings and travellings of the Master, those very close in the family of Lucius also came under the direction of those teachings. Then, with the changes wrought during the periods of the trial, the crucifixion, and then the happenings which came about from the reports spread abroad as to what were the actual conditions existent when the hour of the crucifixion had come, then the third day, and the reports of his rising again, and of his meeting with the disciples at the Sea of Tiberius (or Galilee), and then the ascension upon or from the holy mount, these brought to that family wonderment and interest.

"So, with the repeating of that as had been the experience of the brother, little wonder that the sister was desirous of knowing more of those happenings, desirous of seeing, experiencing, being in contact with individuals who had actually seen and heard the words of the Master, desirous of meeting those who had been healed by the laying on of hands, by merely the word spoken, desirous of hearing those who had eaten of bread created by the word of that Teacher.

"Thus, though young in years, being around sixteen years of age, Nimmuo, with the brother, journeyed to the environs in which those things, those experiences had been an actual, living part of the experience of those many individuals.

"Being in the position of not only being countenanced by but friends of those in authority, though there were questionings, yet there was honor shown these two through their activities in that journey through the Holy Land, across the Sea of Galilee, down those portions of the Jordan, through Perea, to Bethany, into the city itself, the house of Martha and Mary and Lazarus, the acquaintance of the mother, Mary, and the rest of the family that had been gathered by John, then, as in keeping with that command from the cross.

"Each of these individuals heard again and again much of that which has been lost by the attempt of individuals to interpret in the varied tongues." There were the stories told of what had happened in Bethany, "how Mary had been cleansed from those activities and experiences little of which until then had even been spoken of in the presence of Nimmuo." Also, they heard much of Martha, "the one sedate, calm, never venturing to offer her body, ever, in those activities that had made Mary the byword of so many; also those stories as to how word had been sent to the Master as to the illness of Lazarus, his visits, and the eventual bringing forth, after four days in the tomb." They heard of the experiences of Lazarus as he, himself, had given, "as to his experience or consciousness in that period of the inter-between, as to what had happened, as to how there had arisen that consciousness, that movement within, when that voice had called, 'Lazarus, come forth!' "

Then came the day of the Pentecost, when there were the mighty gatherings; when Lucius and Nimmuo and Mariaerh and Eunice and those many peoples beheld in awe the outpouring of the Holy Spirit, when the Spirit "descended as in tongues of fire and sat upon that body of the twelve;" heard that speech of Peter when he spoke in tongues—"or as he spoke in his own tongue," said Cayce, "it, the message, was heard by those of every nation in their own tongue."

These experiences "so impressed Lucius that there came a re-dedicating, and the determination within self to become the closer associated with, the closer affiliated with the disciples or apostles."

"The many of many lands," Cayce continues, "were brought to conviction by the teachings of the apostles on that day, and especially in that memorable one of Peter's." Perhaps the experience of Eunice, into whose life had come so much of disappointment and fear and hate, was typical of these. When she "heard her own kinsmen speak in tongues, seeing the great tumult and the activities wrought," said Cayce, there "was builded that determination within the experience and heart of the woman to bring the greater knowledge, the greater awareness of the spirit of truth, as was indeed manifested by him that shed, through the tenets of his disciples and apostles the new light to men: that hate and those things that make afraid may be put away, and that positions of power or wealth or fame may be set at naught compared to the peace that came and is the understanding of those who

153

have seen and known and become aware of his presence abiding."

When there were the first attempts for organized effort on the part of the teachers or apostles, as is recorded in the book of Acts, all the material belongings of those who joined in this fellowship became as a part of the apostles', and they were "with one accord together." The number of these became exceedingly large, for three thousand were baptized on the first day of the apostles' teaching, and the number was added to daily. It was necessary to choose some people to act as deacons or ministers to the needs of the great throngs of people, or in the words of Cayce, "the distribution of the needs of those that had set themselves and their only worldly goods to be used by those in authority in the church," for many confusions arose.

"There were those," said Cayce, "who were entirely of the circumcision; there were those chosen who were of the uncircumcised group, yet were identified with services in various forms in that which had been adopted by the Samaritan Jews. Some of these facts became problems (that were unnecessary in their particular activity, or for their beliefs) in the teachings of Peter, John, James, who were the chief spokesmen during those periods."

With Stephen, Philip, and others, according to Cayce, there was chosen a young man named Philas who was at the time only a little past nineteen years of age. Philas "was of that group of people from Seleucia who came to Jerusalem during those days of the Pentecost, when there was an outpouring of the Holy Spirit upon the apostles who had been warned to tarry in Jerusalem until that day."

He was among those who were students of the law, those who were interested in the questionings concerning the interpretations of the Mosaic law by the priests and rabbis of the day, and "the interesting facts and fancies

154

that had come from the eastern lands from which the wise men had come. These, as parts of the teachings, had become adopted by those groups of the Essenes of which John and Joseph had been a part before the entering of the Master, Jesus, into the earth."

"Philas was of a group not wholly either Jewish or Grecian, but one interested in same, because of the background, genealogically, of the things happening. He journeyed to Jerusalem because of the interest aroused by hearsay and the expectance among the peoples, the great throngs. As a student he was aroused to the possibilities and probabilities of the activities to which the individuals might give themselves, or contribute to, or gain something from, as to add to the interest in living."

He had not been acquainted, directly, until this period, with the individuals who had been associated with the Master as disciples, now apostles, or those who had been very close in the activity. On the journey to Jerusalem, however, Philas became closely associated with Stephen, who, after the joining of so many to the efforts of the apostles on the day of Pentecost, "became the treasurer of the organization that became a necessity, in that record keepers had to be appointed because of the great amount of contributions of various natures to those peoples."

With the establishing of the church in Jerusalem, Martha, the wife of Nicodemus, "was among those who aided Stephen and Philip, as well as others of various lands. For it was with these that Martha first became acquainted with Luke and Lucius who later became the heads of various organizations in other portions." Stephen was a close friend of Lucius, Luke, "and those of the younger group that became the companions of the teachers." These relationships were in the nature of counsel from Martha, to whom Stephen, Luke, Lucius and Mark, "as the younger of the disciples (not apostles but younger of the disciples) went for counsel." For Martha "was one acquainted with the law," and she taught the law to the young ones, the children who sought knowledge.

When the persecutions began, Martha "withdrew more and more because of the associations with those in authority, but her home became more and more a place of refuge and help for all of the young of the church."

CHAPTER TWO

THE SPREAD OF CHRISTIANITY

The spread of Christian teachings to other lands began with the persecution of the church and the consequent scattering of the believers, the converts. This began as is recorded in the Bible, with the stoning of Stephen and the persecutions led by Saul of Tarsus, when many of the followers of these teachings were thrown into prison.

According to Cayce, Lazarus and his sister Martha were also victims of this persecution. "Lazarus' life," Cayce said, "was only until the first of the rebellions arose, for on his activity much of that which caused the dissension (from the first raising from the dead) was produced in the minds of the people and the experiences of the high priest at the time.

"As to Martha's experience then in this period: With the rebellions that arose (that is, the coming of the soldiery that made for the dissension) we find Martha joined with those that brought the rebellion of Saul; and it was under his direction that the persecutions and banishments brought about the death of Martha."

Several examples are given by Cayce of those who, because of the persecutions and for other reasons, left Jerusalem, bringing the teachings known as the Gospel to those of other areas.

Ulai had become acquainted "with the young converts of the Grecians as well as those in Laodicea, and with the separating of those when persecutions arose and Stephen was stoned" and "with the spread of the teachings as brought about by the breaking up of the Holy Women (of which Ulai was classed, though among the younger of that group) she joined in the church activities in Laodicea."

Nimmuo, the sister of Lucius, had spent most of her stay in Palestine in the company of the Holy Women and their associates, their friends, in and about Jerusalem. Their many stories about the activities, the miracles, the teachings of the Master had brought her an awareness "that was to be a part of Nimmuo's experience during those questionings which arose later in the church in Laodicea." With the scattering of the disciples, the friends, after the death of Stephen, the death of Lazarus, Nimmuo then returned to the home in Laodicea.

With the activities of the deacons of the church "there became for Philas questions with some of the apostles, in that Philas used the position to which he had been appointed as a means for social relationships with the various groups of women, the girls that were a part of the activities through those particular periods. These brought questionings as to the sincerity of purpose in the oaths taken, and the living up to same," because of the seeming negligence concerning these relationships. And this was a problem among many of those in the early church. "For in portions of the land from which Philas came, as in Laodicea, Thyatira, as in all of those where there were the mixed relationships of Greeks, Romans, Jews and Syrophoenicians, there was the following of the eastern tenets of many of those peoples as to their relationships with the opposite sex.

"The greater disturbance arose after the martyrdom of Stephen. This drew Philas closer to the needs of the people, but because of the persecutions many of the groups were scattered throughout the various lands, and Philas returned to his own land, becoming engaged in those activities that brought about a greater contribution."

So the persecutions brought about the spread of what they were intended to stamp out. And the peoples of many lands began to know and to wonder at the teachings of the Nazarene and the faith of his followers.

When or by whom the gospel was first carried to Rome is not known from either the Bible or other historical sources. Apparently there was considerable Christian activity there by the end of the reign of Claudius in 54 A.D., for the statement was made by the Roman writer Suetonius that Claudius expelled the Jews from Rome for rioting "at the instigation of Chrestus (Christ)."*

Possibly the first reports as to the life of Jesus and the Christian activity were those told about by Cayce, at the period when there were "those requirements by those in authority in the experience that Pilate must make a personal report of what took place in that period when a prophet—yea, more than a prophet—was condemned, when one that, by the very voice of many, was known to be of unsavory repute was loosed again in the earth."

One of the individuals responsible for this questioning of Pilate was, according to Cayce, a man known as Cercel, who was in authority in the Roman Empire. He "was not of the household of the Caesars, but of those who were in the relative relationships, as would be termed, and of those who had been given authority by those in office or in power in the period," and "was chosen because of his executive and physical abilities, as well as because of favor bestowed by the parents.

"In his activities Cercel visited many of the lands from which there were customs to be gathered, and counseled not only with those who were set in authority as the judges or the political representatives of the land, but also with those who actually gathered or collected the tribute or tax, and whose activities, in co-ordination or cooperation with Cercel, were to carry that collected to those in authority at Rome."

---

* James L. Price. *Interpreting the New Testament*

These lands governed by Rome at this period were "much of that adjacent to the Mediterranean: Rome, Sicily, Mesopotamia or Turkey, Greece, Palestine, and all of northern Africa and southern Europe, as called in the present."

Cercel's extensive travels made it possible for him to study in "the great library . . . in what is now known as Alexandria, where there had been the gatherings of data by the sages of old. For all of those influences and forces, not only of the Egyptians and the Persians and the lands beyond the seas, but the activities in many other lands (as the prophecies concerning the coming of the Messiah in Palestine) were included in the records there," and these became a part of Cercel's study.

Thus, when he journeyed into the Palestine land, after the crucifixion of the Master, there was the understanding, the harkening to "the cries from some of the individuals who were associated with Cercel in the collecting of taxes, and the demand of some that there be a questioning of Pilate by Caesar as related to those things which had come about."

Philoas was apparently one of those associated with Cercel, for it was primarily through the activity and demands of Philoas, Cayce says, that Pilate was called to Rome for questioning, and Philoas then made his own report concerning the arrest and crucifixion.

"For, as the representative of the government, Philoas then was acting in the capacity of one who looked upon the abilities of groups, of individuals, not as a spy, but rather as an analyst of their relationship under a divided spiritual and political rule. For he looked not only to their patriotism (as would be termed in the present) to the Roman land, but also to the interests of the people. Not as one that considered only those in authority, of high estate, but rather as man to man, as were the real purposes of the Roman rule in these experiences," and that the dictates of the local rulers "were to be carried not to

160

the extremes," but as considered reasonable by those in power, in position. These made for the activity of Philoas as one in authority higher than the local government or the protectorate or any other influence.

These, then, were the background as shown by Philoas' report to Caesar:

"Those activities of Herod, that was as the local representative of the peoples in their religious thought, their religious intent, their religious claim, as may be said.

"Then the authority as given to the protectorate, or the proletariat, as would be termed, for the civil government, law, order. And that condition which existed between the two, as Philoas had set in motion: that not only was the tribute to be collected by the Roman citizenry, but also was there to be kept, to be created, to be made the more perfect understanding, not only of the protectorate as to the religious forces of the Jews, but also as to their political forces and influences. And yet these (Herod and the protectorate) had built many experiences that made for the condemning of same" because of the differences that arose between them and altered much of that intended to be as coordinating activities.

"Then there came the time when there was the report to be made by Philoas upon those happening there upon the hill of shame, upon the cross. And there was the command that there be a report of the civil ruler, Pilate, before the emperor, the physical king."

"When there was the recalling of Pilate, and the reports that had been made as to the activities of the wife of Pilate as related to the healing that had been accomplished in the household, then we find a report [made by Philoas] very favorable to the Christians, though he was questioned much by those who were directly under his supervision." He was "not condemned by those that knew; condemned rather by those who became fearful of the change in the social order of the day—not by those in authority civilly, or by those in authority from the religious point of view, but rather the social."

At this hearing, Phlons, who "was among those of the soldiery of Pilate that ruled in Judea and Jerusalem," and who had cast his lot with those people who followed the Prince of Peace, presented to Caesar the activities of Pilate at the trial, as well as those of the high priest in the condemning of Jesus; for Phlons had been among those who stood guard at the time of the crucifixion, and had seen the Prince of Peace die on the cross, and harkened back "to a day when the sun was darkened, and not by an eclipse alone, and when the earth shook and the temple veil was rent; for he viewed these experiences in the affairs of men." And so he testified.

Mathias was another "brought as one of those who would bear witness as to the activities of Pilate during the trial of the man called Jesus. He was in that position of attempting to fulfill his own ideas as to the interpretation of the law, as well as the attempt to be upon the right terms with those who by force had brought him to Rome for the testimony. Thus he was drawn between two fires—that as whether to be true to his religion, or to that aş might bring into the experience favor with those in authority."

Then, though Philoas's report was questioned by many, it was accepted by the Roman emperor, and acted upon according to Philoas's recommendations—"that Pilate be removed, and one closer in sympathy with the Christian movement be appointed in the stead, as is seen, or is recorded, by profane history, as well as by intimation in sacred history."

"Philoas, then, may be said to have been the influence even greater than the apostle Paul in bringing to the Roman conscience a correct report of what happened in Jerusalem—yea, and in Galilee and Samaria."

Later Philoas "returned to Rome as one that counseled with the Caesars concerning these very activities, and making the changes that brought Philip and Agrippa to power, and the judges that were to judge later in those periods in which Paul, Peter and John were active. Though remaining a Roman, he was in sympathy with those activities, lending counsel and giving those influences that prevented the full destruction of the disciples during those periods of experience."

Aquilasteben was among those Roman soldiers garrisoned in the Holy Land during that period when the Master walked in the earth, and had been among those "seeking for the knowledge of those activities carried on by the Master, as well as the disciples." He had sought out the Master, "coming in contact with same through the offices of Mary, Martha, John, and James." Thus he had contributed "not only in the material needs and activities, but in the actual bringing of a greater understanding to many of the peoples through those trials, through those persecutions" which followed the establishing of the church. Because of this activity, Acquilasteban was recalled to Rome. Yet he was active, even there, and aided those who brought the tenets and truths to Rome.

At that time when there was the great persecution of the church a Jerusalem, especially by Saul, the learned and prominent Pharisee, and by the orthodox religious rulers, and there was thus the scattering abroad of those more active in the church, except the apostles, there was also the beginning of the missionary activities—the fulfilling of that command: "Go ye into all the world and preach the gospel . . . baptizing them in the name of the Father and of the Son and of the Holy Ghost."

Then Philip, having preached in the city of Samaria, as recorded in Acts, performing many miracles and baptizing the many who believed, returned to that area to the south of Jerusalem; and there came that experience when there was the meeting with the eunuch from Ethiopia, on the road from Jerusalem to Gaza.

This man, according to Cayce, was named Euendi, and was "a ruler in the Ethiopian land, an emissary to those people of the Queen Candace, and came [to the Holy Land] for political reasons . . . when he came directly under the influence of Philip and accepted those teachings." And when he returned to his own land, said Cayce, many of his political accomplishments were in accordance with that light, that knowledge gained by that experience by the way.

"And there may yet be uncovered in the Ethiopian land the records made by this entity of the teachings of Philip and Simon in that land. For these are among the purest records, for they were written not only on papyrus that is of the better character, but in the Ethiopian land the conditions were such that it still remains intact, this record of the experience of Euendi meeting Philip, and as to what were the words and teachings of Jesus of Nazareth."

With the persecutions that had arisen against that now known as the church, Lucius of Cyrene was rejected as one of those "who were to act as those called the deacons, as Philip and Stephen and the others . . . because of his close associations with one later called Paul, or Saul; he [Saul] being also of Tarsus, or of the country, and a Roman, and questioned as to his Jewish ancestry . . . though claimed by Paul that he was a Jew. His mother was, indeed, and of the tribe of Benjamin, though his father was not.

"Hence the questions arose as to the advisability of putting those in positions either as teachers, ministers, or those in active service, that were questioned as to their lineal descent. And again the old question as to whether any were to receive the word but those of the household of faith, or the Jews."

Apparently the more fearful in this regard were overruled, for Lucius soon became quite active in the affairs of the church.

During the days in which Mariaerh had remained in or about Jerusalem as a friend, a guest of Martha and Mary and Lazarus, she became closely associated with Lucius, who also was entertained by the sisters and Lazarus at this period. And after the establishing of the church, when Mariaerh had been among the first ten to be baptized, her "activities and associations with Lucius became as those close activities for the founding of the ministry, the missionary activities, the influences that brought about the establishing of many portions of the church during that early ministry of not only the apostles, but those early ministers of the church, as Mark and Luke and Lucius and all of those . . . Thaddeus and Saul or Paul, and Barnabas and those of Laodicea."

"There is often the confusing of Lucius and Luke," Cayce says, "for these were kinsmen (Luke being the brother of Lucius' mother, Mercedon), and Lucius and Luke were drawn or thrown together, and with the conversion of Saul, or Paul as he became, they followed closer and closer with the activities of Paul."

Peter, it is related by the writer of Acts, journeyed about Judea, doing miracles of healing, whereby many were converted and baptized. Then, when Cornelius of Caesarea, having been instructed in a vision, sent messengers to bring Peter to him, he came and preached the Gospel to him and his household.

One of that household was, according to Cayce, named Celicene, "the elder daughter of the ruler or judge or proconsul of the actions connected with the Roman soldiery; for Cornelius was in the office of all of these in Caesarea.

"Though born in Rome, she came early in the life into that environ, in which the surroundings were such as to make for the understanding that differences existed in the lives of the individuals around her. Hence, the early life brought those conditions in which there was the feeling in her experience of being above most of those about her, or that they were somewhat inferior. This is not in nature of criticism, for the environs and conditions which existed caused such a feeling.

"Then, with the changes which came about because of the conversion of Cornelius, and the association of his household with the disciples, the change in Celicene was not so quick. Neither was there the absorbing, wholly, of the ideas presented by those teachers who, to Celicene, in the most part appeared to be rather uncouth, or men who were not of the same estate, or class, or group as she, herself. Yet she sought and desired, because of the sincerity of those of the household, to be in accord with that being practiced as a part of the experience of the household.

"Hence, no wonder that there were turmoils in the inner feelings, the inner emotions of the entity. For there were the social and economic changes which were naturally wrought by those of the household becoming so absorbed as to make the home a place where there were the meetings of various groups."

There was also a confusion which arose during that period in Celicene's attempt "to unify the teachings of Paul and the teachings of Peter who was, to her parent, the confessor. There was a great variation. One held that the body must be under surveillance at all times. The other held that the use of the offices of the body, whether physical, social, or material, were not to be considered so much, just so the mind was kept in accord."

Though Luke and Lucius became very good frends of Celicene during those experiences, Paul became rather that one who, to her, "brought those turmoils, because of his manner of presentation to the various groups.

"For remember, as indicated here," Cayce points out, the followers and disciples and teachers or ministers who were in the position of the Roman citizens did not always hold the same tenets as the ones who were of the house-

166

hold of the Jews. "Remember, there was a vast difference in the teachings, even of the leaders."

No wonder, then, that in the present one may find hard to correlate the writings of some of those "who attempted to present their understanding, and a variation as to just what Peter meant as expressed in Mark, in Luke, or by Paul."

"Peter, Paul, Luke, Mark, Lucius, *all* were men, with appetites, desires, that sought their indulgence oft, and gave expressions to same and these, with the various groups produced the turmoils."

Yet the turmoils, the problems arising in the experience of any may be met in these manners: though "each phase of an entity's personality, individuality, has of itself its own questions, its own problems, yet they are all answered in that oneness of purpose, oneness of desire that the body, the mind, the soul, be in accord, in attune, with that as He would have thee be! For He never condemned any."

"Later in the experience, when the activities brought about the greater associations with those of her own peoples in the Roman Land, Celicene found that answer as has been indicated; and thus she brought constructive experiences through her activities throughout the sojourn there, and brought the greater blessings to those with whom she came in contact."

She "saw the phenomena in the household of Cornelius," in the servants, in her own parents, which she sought and yet never fully experienced. She learned later, it was not necessary that she speak with tongues, "but with that tongue of love, which is the language of all who seek His face."

After the conversion of Saul and his joining with those who held to the Christian beliefs or tenets, there appears to have been little organized persecution of the church for a period of several years. Then began the persecution by the Herodians, who "during that portion," according

167

to Cayce, "had held to the mixing of the blood of the human with that of the sacrifice."

James, the brother of the Lord, had been "raised to that position as head of the church through the direct influence of James and John, the sons of Zebedee. This brought about that first of the authorities putting forth their hands and slaying James [the son of Zebedee] by the sword. This happened, not by that of trial, but by that as would be called a riot; and not incorrectly were James and John called the sons of thunder."

Sarapha "was first among those to suffer martyrdom by the roughness of the Romans that attempted to disperse the crowds. For, through the injuries that came, broken of body, she suffered in the flesh." Yet still Sarapha looked ever "to Him who is Life, Light and Immortality to those who put their trust wholly in Him."

Sofa, also, was "among those first disturbed by the first edicts that brought death to James, dying in that period from exposure by the abuse of the soldiers in that first raid."

Josie also "passed on through those periods of riot following the beheading of James."

When Peter, then, was arrested and thrown into prison, as recorded in Acts, it is little wonder that there was little hope held for his life. Yet a number of the followers gathered with prayer and weeping in the home of John Mark, for many of these, according to Cayce, were kinsmen: Marcus, who was the father of John Mark and the nephew of Peter and Andrew; Cleopas, the father of Marcus and the brother-in-law of Peter; Josie, the wife of Marcus and the sister of Mary, the mother of Jesus; and Mary and Rhoda, the sisters of Mark.

When the knocking came upon the door, and Rhoda, hearing and recognizing the voice of Peter, ran to tell the others that Peter was there, they could not believe. It was, said Cayce, a man named Clement, "in the household of James the Less, the brother of the Lord," who "opened the door when Peter knocked, astonished as the rest."

When, as we are told in Acts, those present in the house had been told of the happenings in the prison, how the light had shone and the chains had fallen from his hands and he had been led from the prison through open doors, still believing it to be a dream until he found himself free upon the street, and when instructions had been given as to messages to be sent to others of the brethren, Peter departed from Jerusalem and went down, for a time, to Caesarea.

When there was, according to Cayce, the dispersing of the followers, "the spread of the teachings by the persecutions in Jerusalem when James was beheaded . . . Andrew and Bartholomew chose to go towards the east rather than the west," and, accompanied by a disciple named Pebelus, they went into Mesopotamia and Persia and those countries where Andrew "felt that the learning of the Master was obtained during the early education and travels of the Master."

"Then Andrew," Cayce said, "remained true to that teaching, and brought many to the knowledge of God that is within every human physical being that seeks to know how God manifests through the individual."

Saul and Barnabas also left Jerusalem, taking with them John, whose surname was Mark; going first to Antioch where Lucius of Cyrene then ministered, then traveling through much of the surrounding country, carrying the gospel and establishing churches in many places; and Mark acted as secretary to Barnabas.

One of these areas was that of Laodicea, from which Lucius and his sister had come and to which many of the disciples had gone when the persecutions had begun —Laodicea, that became the scene of some of the bitterest dissension that arose in the early church.

169

CHAPTER THREE

DISSENSION IN THE CHURCH

The book of Acts and the letters of Paul reveal only occasional hints of dissension in the church, and none of any disturbances in the church in Laodicea. Indeed, there are only a few brief references to the Laodiceans to be found in the New Testament, other than that in Revelation. According to Cayce, however, the activities at Laodicea, centering around Lucius, his wife, and a woman named Vesta, had a great deal to do with some of Paul's teachings and attitudes. They also indicate that these early Christian leaders, saints though they may have been, had many of the same weaknesses and problems that beset the church today.

"As may be found in the records, or recorded history," Cayce says, "there had been those journeyings of the peoples of the families of the Caesars to what was then the area around Laodicea." Among these was Vesta, a young woman, part Grecian yet considered a Roman, as her father, Xeren, was a Roman citizen. She was "not of the Caesars that were in power or authority, but of the household of the cousins . . . and in the position to draw upon the influences of the court, as well as the established places of activity of the empire then—through Macedonia, through Greece, through Palestine, through the North African land."

The influences during the earlier portion of her life, therefore, were the customs of the Grecian and the Roman, but "as the influence of the Christian faith began to be noted in the land" she came in contact "with those who were as the missionaries, or those who had been set in authority over the churches or places of Christian activity. Though in the secular forces she was averse to such affairs, she acted in the capacity of one who looked upon the activities of those for the reporting; or as ye would term such an activity in the present, she was in a diplomatic service or activity."

In this way she "became associated especially with Lucius," who was associated with "those activities in Macedonia, in Mesopotamia, and in the northern portions of the Palestine land."

Through "the association with individuals who had, in a manner, adopted the Christian, or the Jewish and Christian faith," and particularly with Lucius, "there came the adopting of some of the customs of these." And yet, though "there had been the making of the marriage agreement or contract for Lucius," this had little effect upon the companionship or associations of these two. "For there were children born to these through those associations in the early part of that activity."

"When there were those acceptances by Lucius, Luke, and the Laodiceans, or Grecians and Romans, to journey to the Holy Land, or to Jerusalem, these brought disputations." But "during that experience [in Jerusalem] the marriage took place between the contracting parties, Lucius, who had been Vesta's companion, and Mariaerh," who had been a part of the activities in the earlier portion of the Jerusalem experience.

In the meantime, changes were coming about also, in the attitudes and understandings of the family of Lucius.

Nimmuo, the sister of Lucius, who had returned to her home in Laodicea at the time of the first persecutions of the church "became for the time an enigma to the mother, Sophia, and to the father Philippi, who, not until the teachings or the ministry of Paul, understood or interpreted aright Nimmuo's attempt to give the better or greater impressions of what had been received by the visit to Jerusalem and those happenings there. Much of this, of course, was owing to the circumstances, as might be said, of that day and period.

"Yet, with the coming of Paul and Barnabas, there was in the house of Philippi a great awakening to those possibilities as being presented by the whole acceptance of those teachings—the teachings of the Master, who had given so full and complete an interpretation of God as the Father, God as Love, God as Patience, God as Long-suffering.

"Then more and more were the other disciples frequenting those portions of the land, as they were scattered more and more by the edicts that had been brought about in the church in Jerusalem."

"With the acceptance of Lucius by Paul, and part of those in the Caesarean church, Lucius determined, with his companion, to return to the portion of his own land, and to there attempt to establish a church; to be the minister, to be the active force in those portions of the land."

When the church was established, then, in Laodicea, "Lucius was made . . . by Paul and Barnabas . . . head (or Bishop) of the church."

There were several women who were said by Cayce to have had an active position in the church at Laodicea. Apparently Paul's ban on women's taking an active part was not yet in effect or did not influence this particular church.

Josida, who had heard Peter on the day of Pentecost, was later among those scattered with the early persecutions of "the Romans who were sent to replace the centurion at Antioch"; thus "became a follower of Paul and Barnabas into Laodicea, and became an active influence there, being the lady superior, or mother of the church there, growing under the activities of the members of . . . what was later called the Presbytery of that particular group of individuals."

Susane was "established as one of the first deaconesses

of that church." And Ulai, also, "joined in the church activities in Laodicea."

As the bishop of the church, "or the director, or the president of the presbytery, or what ye would call the priest, or the father, or the high counselor, as given to those in the early periods of the church," Lucius became "the one to whom all questions were taken respecting what ye, in the present, would term theology, or questions pertaining to the law. In such the bishop was the last word, other than that there might be the appeal from such a verdict to the church in Jerusalem, or the apostles themselves.

"Such disputes brought disturbances at times, especially when there were the questionings as Paul brought into that region as to whether it was well for those in such positions (that is, as the bishops or leaders in the church) to be married or not. And the declaration as made through the Corinthian and the Ephesian letters* indicate what disturbances there were; because differences arose between Lucius and Paul, as well as between Silas and Paul and Barnabas and those that had become the leaders, or the real ministers or missionaries for the church."

There were "questionings as to the experience of Vesta and the disputations that later arose as to the associations . . . with those in the church."

"For many—many—questioned the purposes of Vesta with Lucius."

"The disputations arose especially with Paul. For Paul sided with Vesta in the periods when, for eighteen months, he remained in Laodicea to build up, or strengthen, the church. Yet Barnabas, who had been of the combinations that guided the offices of the church, had sided with those of Lucius' household."

"Nimmuo, having known, having heard, much of what had been given by Martha, by Mary, by Lazarus, by

* See especially II Corinthians, Chapters 11 and 12.

173

John and the other disciples, felt for and sided with that royal personage (Vesta)." Thus she, Nimmuo, "was thrown or drawn into a disturbance that made for those activities in which another (Ulai) brought about what was almost the dividing of the church in Laodicea, and caused that saint in Patmos to declare, 'I will spue thee out.' "*

For "with what was termed by some the faithlessness of Lucius, and preached so, even by Paul, Ulai almost renounced all, and brought about what might be called the first separation in the church in Laodicea. Because of her activities, differences spread in many of the churches, not only in the local activities around Laodicea, but in Antioch and in Phrygia, Jerusalem and Patmos."

Then came "the teachings of Paul concerning the interests of those who were as leaders or the heads of the churches, and from which grew in many quarters the commanding or demanding of celibacy as a prerequisite for the activities as a bishop or leader.

"This caused Mariaerh, owing to the fact that there were no children, to feel that most of those teachings of Paul—or many—were directed at her," and "made for periods when there was the withdrawing of the companion [of Lucius] and her closer association with the teacher that had been the proclaimer and the director in the early experience of the life of the Master himself—or with Judy —and with Elizabeth and with Mary, the mother of the Lord."

Then, when there were "the close friendships that grew between John Mark and Mariaerh, again questions arose in the minds of many, owing to the differences in ages between Lucius and Mariaerh. These caused many disturbing conditions."

Eventually Nimmuo, with the aid of her mother "brought about order, discipline, even treading where

* Revelation 4:16

174

others would have feared to undertake to admonish those who were the superiors as to positions in the church. For Nimmuo admonished those who were many years the senior. But, having received that conviction, that purpose, that ideal, from those experiences in Bethany in the home of the mother of the Lord, in John's home, as well as in that experience on the day of Pentecost, Nimmuo stood as a mighty power, alone with the Truth in the lack of condemnation to any."

"With those experiences, and with Paul's being carried on in his second missionary journey, and with many of the things propounded by him that Lucius had declared as things that were unstable, there again—with the teachings to Mariaerh by Judy, by the mother of the Lord, and Elizabeth, in their years of maturity teaching this younger person, there was brought that which John proclaimed: that there is in the church in Laodicea no fault, yet it is neither hot nor cold, and for the lack of its very stand it would find condemning."

"With the settling of conditions, "or the disputes that had arisen, Vesta "began her active work among the peoples in that particular land. The activities that had been a part of her experience in early childhood then began to show expression. Thus, her influence with the young, her special interest and feeling for children, then brought an activity in the directing of same . . . in directing the activity of the youth in every form, as of weaving, knitting, dancing, basket weaving, applique work, tent making"—all of these were a part of her activities. She "lived to be a deaconess in the church in Laodicea," and there was a close activity with Luke "in aiding in the writing, and what might be called the reporting of the activities of the church to Luke, and also to John. For Vesta was associated with John, the beloved, in the periods before he was sent to Patmos, as an old man; and it was under his influence and direction that Vesta was made deaconess in the church. Her associations with Luke were

175

those because of the close friendship between Luke and Lucius, whom Vesta never lost contact with through the experience."

Although the only contact she had had with Jesus had been "as the experience through the visions and through the close associations with those who had been with him, these had been explained, these had been developed, so that the visions became as realities, "as they may be, said Cayce, "to all who will to be one with Him, and act in love to make same possible."

Soon after the disputes in Laodicea, there came another incident which later became the cause or the source of conflict and disagreement between Paul and Barnabas, and this was concerning John Mark. For he, Mark, as related in Acts, left them at Perga and returned to Jerusalem. For this, his desertion, he was criticized much by Paul, and, according to Cayce, "questioned oft by the superiors as one not well grounded in faith," but Barnabas was more tolerant of the weakness, the timidity, the fearfulness of this young man.

John Mark had first entered into that experience, Cayce says, "during that period when there were turmoils among the peoples of which he was a part, and while still young in years saw much of the oppression of peoples for the thought as held." For he "was born during that period which would be known as the sixteenth year of our Lord," the son of Josie and Marcus, "close to and a relative of Chloe and Lois, [they and] Josie all relatives of Mary, the mother of the Lord, of the tribe of Judah, of the household of Marcus; hence, sometimes referred to as Marcus, or son of Marcus."

In his twelfth year he had been "healed from an infirmity by the associations with John, the cousin of the Lord, and the Lord." For "he was lame in the left limb, and healed by, first, the approaching of John called the

Baptist; later, he was healed entirely by the Master during the first year of his ministry."

When Paul began his second missionary journey with Barnabas, according to the Bible, Barnabas would have again had Mark accompany them; but Paul's attitude of condemnation toward Mark, and his refusal to allow again this association brought about the separation of Paul and Barnabas. Saul, then, chose Silas to accompany him, while Mark accompanied Barnabas in his ministry, or missionary activities.

According to Cayce, the faith of Barnabas in Mark was fully justified; for though he had been "in young manhood . . . among those that were fearful," he gained "in stamina and strength as persecutions became greater."

"He assisted Barnabas in the establishing of the church in northern Africa, or Alexandria, where so much persecution later was shown in the activities in that center. Much that was compiled by Mark in this land was destroyed in or during the second century. This had been compiled in the great library in Alexandria. There are still intact some of the writings that may yet be reclaimed in some of the ruins about the place, as well as in some of those cities in Chaldea and Persia, where Mark, in the last days went in company with Andrew."

"As yet there are little of the writings of letters of John Mark, or son of Marcus, other than that contained in the gospel known as Mark."

"In poetry there was little save the reconstruction of some of the psalms that were used in the dedicating of those places of meeting, and in the services at times in these various places."

The Gospel of Mark was written "in collaboration with Peter and Barnabas. This was the first of the written words respecting the acts, the life, the deeds of the Master. While it is shorter in words, there is more in body content of the acts than in most of the other writings. It is nearer in accord with that in Matthew, but not an

177

abridged writing; for Matthew was written from the churches in Pamphilia, while Mark wrote from Rome." The Gospel of Mark "was written during the fifty-ninth year, or during the thirty-fourth year of Mark's experience in that plane," while that of Matthew "was written some ten to eighteen years later."

Mark was often "a companion with Luke, who was an associate and companion of Paul oft in his travels. Luke, being of those people that were free, as he was not of the Jewish descent, thus aided John Mark in his abilities to go and come rather at ease; hence, after becoming more stable than as a young man, he was of so much more aid to the peoples during that period," suffering much in many ways, afflicted in body, yet gaining throughout "in the service rendered to many."

CHAPTER FOUR

THE OPPOSITION OF ROME

The primary causes of the opposition of Rome to the Christian movement is not clear from either sacred or profane history. The "Annals" of the Roman historian Tacitus state that Nero, after the disastrous fire in Rome in A.D. 65, made a scapegoat of the Christians, accusing them of setting the fire that destroyed a large portion of the city, to dispel the rumor that he himself had started the conflagration to make way for the enlargement of his palace and gardens. However, according to Tacitus, the Christians were already hated, and were convicted "not so much on the charge of arson as because of their hatred of humanity."

James Price, in *Interpreting the New Testament*, suggests the possibility that Paul's trial in Rome, the publicity and investigation caused by his appeal to Rome, may have affected the attitude of the Roman people towards Christianity.

There is no doubt as to the fact of the massacre itself in A.D. 65, when large numbers of Christians were brutally destroyed and Christianity officially outlawed by Nero.

There is an ancient church tradition that both Peter and Paul were martyred in Rome at this time, Peter being crucified with his head downward. This is not historically certain, nor is it reported in the New Testament. A letter written from Rome by Clement about A.D. 96 gives the earliest Christian report of the Martyrdom of Peter and Paul. The reasons given in this letter for their deaths are "rivalry and envy," "wicked jealousy," and "rivalry and contention." Price believes that these words suggest conflict within the church at Rome as a possible factor in the attack on Christianity.

The Cayce readings shed more light on this question, as well as relating the fate of other apostles and disciples.

"In the persecutions and the changes," Cayce said, "that came about in the individual authorities in the various provinces [of the Roman Empire], Philoas returned again and again to those lands, associations, and activities, meeting with those who had been the keepers of the records here or there, those who had been in authority for the levying of taxes, the manners of the levying, and the like." And "all was in purpose, in desire, to be even as he, the Master taught: that they who for any cause lord over their fellow man become that as must sooner or later become a stumbling stone."

Thus, "throughout Philoas' experience and associations with those of what ye call or term the Palestine experience, there was no rebellion of those peoples of the land against Roman authority, only after those periods when Philoas was recalled, or attempted to keep closer in touch with those who had been called to Rome, when Paul, by his own self, brought misinterpreting, misunderstanding." Then "the persecutions of the church arose through the activities of the enmity aroused against Paul, and his disputes with the mother church, or the first church in Antioch and the first church in Jerusalem, headed by the brother of the Lord, James, and Peter and Andrew and the others that from time to time made those visitations there."

During this period of persecution, when many were imprisoned and died, Peter, who during the latter portion of that experience had been teaching in the catacombs of "the Eternal City," as it was then termed, or of Rome, "was crucified with his head downward."

Polias, a sister to Peter's wife, and a follower of Peter, was "among those of the womenfolk who followed those that were imprisoned during those periods, who were forced to give account of the activities before those in power." She "suffered in body and mind," yet "gained . . . that understanding . . . that those of the physical must be crucified that the spiritual life may be made alive."

John also was imprisoned, and here Philoas, "in the last acts of his intervention, saved that apostle for the followers, for the world, from that death as the others had drawn, or had come to.

"Hence the banishment of John was by the very direct intervention of Philoas with those in authority; and the taking away from the churches that had been established in the various places, the records for same, that these might be preserved, became a portion of Philoas' activity."

During those periods of persecutions, John Mark "became a helpmeet to many of the early martyrs, suffering martyrdom himself in the latter portion of the experience at that time; being, however, the martyrdom of expulsion, and traveling in the latter portion of the experience—after the writings in Rome—to those eastern lands with Andrew, the brother of Peter, who had escaped from those same characters of martyrdoms as befell those that had been sent on to Rome." Mark was "sent by Peter and Paul as an emissary to carry the messages of Peter and Paul to those people Andrew was ministering to, in what is now called Persia, aiding oft in the strengthening of the brethren in the various centers where churches or established organizations had been builded by the efforts of Paul, Barnabas, Silas, and the other ministers during that period."

"Once, just before the interventions, Philoas went to the libraries in Alexandria . . . and there were the attempts to placate any of the destructions that later became the loss to what is now called the Christian world."

The "information [that had been] gained from the keeper of the records of the Essenes, Judy, were those things that prompted him . . . to investigate for self those records that were reported to have been made, and that

181

were in the library of Alexandria, of the wise men that came from the other lands just before the birth [of Jesus], and at the time of the birth . . . or a few days later . . . presented themselves in the town of Bethlehem."

"There was the passing, then, from the physical activity in Rome, during that period when there were just the beginnings of the attempts for the unifications of the religious as well as the penal laws, or the laws in the other lands ruled by the Roman Empire." This was "at that age or period some sixty years after the crucifixion . . . then ninety years, or ninety three years of age."

"He passed on naturally, yet losing much in the strength through privation of self that there might be help to those condemned later." For "had he not seen Him (the Lord) entering there and giving that command, 'Ye must stand in my and thy brother's stead, for as they do it unto thy brethren, they do it unto me?' "

As to the latter activities of Ruth, the wife of Philoas, the sister of the Master—"with the changing scenes in Rome, with the death of His representatives, with those in political and religious authority in her own land, then with those changes came the checking up on those that had become imbued with the spirit of these new teachings. Yet her light was not hid under a bushel, but the quietness, the gentleness, the patience [that He taught] was shown in her activities, even in the courts of Bacchus and those revelries that were brought to bear, that there might be a satisfying and a gratifying of the material appetites of men and women during those periods that were, to her, debaucheries. As she looked on these she saw, not the vileness, the flow of those influences of wine and strong drink that excited the passions of men; but rather did she see the blood of her brother spilled in a wanton manner, that the earth might know that he lived not in vain!"

For "during those periods when there had been a relating of that walk to Emmaus . . . there had been the conviction brought that this, indeed, was the son of a living

God." And "those that honor, those that love Him, even as He loved the world, would give, do give their own heart's blood that the world may know that He *lives,* and is at the right hand of the Father, that ye—yea, thy brethren, thy friends, thy enemies—may have an advocate before the Throne of mercy, pleading the cause of the wayward, hearing the cry of those that are persecuted, and saying, 'Be patient—be patient, my child; for in patience know ye thine own soul!' "

APPENDIX

Much of the material from the Cayce readings used in this book was taken from the series of readings #262, #5749, #254 and #364.

The life readings used, with the names given as those of the individuals in that period, are as follows:

#1908	Achlar	#451	Jodie
#1000	Adahr	#1859	Joel
#603	Agatha	#452	John Mark
#2166	Ananan	#1688	Josida
#649	Andra	#1010	Josie
#341	Andrew	#1472	Judy
#1222	Anna	#1924	Lazarus
#2408	Anna	#2823	Lucia
#1196	Apsafar	#294	Lucius
#2803	Aquilasteban	#1968	Maipah
#2549	Ardoen	#1468	Mariaerh
#256	Ashtucil	#295	Mary Magdalene
#2124	Bartimaeus	#2946	Mary—the other Mary
#2205	Celicene	#1974	Mathias
#877	Cercel	#2474	Merceden
#1715	Clement	#540	Naomi
#2154	Cleo	#2677	Nicholas
#870	Cleopas	#2390	Nimmuo
#1207	Cleopeo	#2775	Pebelus
#587	Edithia	#3344	Philas
#1877	Elcor	#1151	Philoas
#1391	Eloise	#333	Phlons
#1541	Esdrela	#1742	Polias
#315	Euendi	#1220	Puloaus
#1602	Eunice	#1217	Romoluon
#1158	Ruth	#1986	Thelda

#1152	Sarapha	#2067	Thesea
#2520	Shalmar	#993	Ulai
#2550	Sodaphe	#1523	Vesta
#2175	Sofa	#1851	Zacheus
#2425	Sophie	#420	Zebedee
#1179	Susane	#2880	Zermada
#1301	Sylvia		

THE A.R.E. TODAY

Out of the wealth of material in the Cayce files grew the Association for Research and Enlightenment, Inc,, and its affiliated organizations, the A.R.E. Press and the Edgar Cayce Foundation.

The Foundation is engaged in the complicated task of indexing and cross-indexing the hundreds of subjects discussed in the readings. Because of their age, the papers are rapidly deteriorating, and they are now being microfilmed for safekeeping and duplicated for ready reference. The subject matter almost blankets the field of human thought; from the value of peanuts to the building of the Great Pyramid; from how to get rid of pinworms to prophecy of the future.

The Association for Research and Enlightenment is an open-membership, nonprofit organization chartered under the laws of the Commonwealth of Virginia to carry on psychic research. It is devoted to the study of the readings and conducts numerous experiments in psychic phenomena. It also cooperates in the field of medicine, psychology and theology. The active membership of the A.R.E., as it is usually called, is made up of people of all religious faiths and many nationalities, including foreign countries. Strangely, they all seem to be able to reconcile their faiths with the philosophy emerging from the Cayce readings. They come from all walks of life; there are doctors, lawyers, ministers, artists, businessmen, teachers, students, working people, housewives.

The Association, governed by a board of trustees, conducts conferences at the Virginia Beach headquarters and regional conferences in New York, Dallas, Denver, Los Angeles and other large cities.

The Association and its affiliated organizations occupy

a large, rambling, three-story frame building of shore architecture. Standing on the highest elevation at Virginia Beach, the building and grounds take up a full city block and face the Atlantic Ocean, a block away. A new building has been constructed which houses a lecture hall, class rooms, offices and the A.R.E. Press.

Hundreds of visitors come every year. With the steadily growing membership and interest, a growing staff handles volumes of inquiries, special requests, lecture announcements and literature. Visitors are shown about the plant and grounds with its broad, tiled veranda overlooking the ocean. The library containing indexed copies of 97% of the readings is of special interest.

To the skeptic there is an appropriate answer: in the words of Abraham Lincoln, "No man has a good enough memory to be a successful liar!" for forty-three years.

—END—

EDGAR CAYCE ON E.S.P.

by Doris Agee

under the editorship of Hugh Lynn Cayce

The definitive work on the celebrated prophet's extraordinary achievements in parapsychological phenomena. ESP topics covered include: out-of-body travel; unusual incidences of clairvoyance; auras; telepathy; missing persons; precognition and prophecy; dreams; psychic development in individuals . . . every aspect of Extrasensory Perception!

☐ (64-122, 75¢)

EDGAR CAYCE ON RELIGION AND PSYCHIC EXPERIENCE

by Harmon Hartzell Bro, Ph.D.

In this illuminating book Dr. Harmon Bro shows, through a detailed analysis of the Cayce readings, that such experiences as

★ using hunches for guidance
★ reading auras
★ communicating with the dead
★ remembering past incarnations

can become as natural as breathing to the person growing spiritually.

☐ (65-216, 95¢)

EDGAR CAYCE ON THE DEAD SEA SCROLLS

by Glenn D. Kittler

under the editorship of Hugh Lynn Cayce

Before the discovery of the Dead Sea Scrolls, no acknowledged expert in history or religion ever put forth the possibility that Jesus, Mary, Joseph, John the Baptist, and other leading figures in the Gospels were associated in any way with the Essenes. Yet for over twenty years, the Life Readings given by Edgar Cayce had been producing information regarding the association.

☐ (65-494, 95¢)

EDGAR CAYCE
ON THE DEAD
SEA SCROLLS

By GLENN D. KITTLER

Under the Editorship of Hugh Lynn Cayce

Before the discovery of the Dead Sea Scrolls, no acknowledged expert in history or religion ever put forth the possibility that Jesus, Mary, Joseph, John the Baptist, and other leading figures in the Gospels were associated in any way with the Essenes. Yet for over twenty years, the Life Readings given by Edgar Cayce had been producing information regarding the association.

(65-494, 95¢)
